Divorced Parenting

Divorced Parenting
How To Make It Work

DR SOL GOLDSTEIN

Methuen London

First published in Canada in 1982
by McGraw-Hill Ryerson Limited
Published in Great Britain in 1987
by Methuen London Ltd,
11 New Fetter Lane, London EC4P 4EE
Copyright © 1982, 1984 by Dr Sol Goldstein

Made and Printed in Great Britain by
Redwood Burn Ltd, Trowbridge, Wiltshire

British Library Cataloguing in Publication Data

Goldstein, Sol
    Divorced parenting: how to make it work.
    1. Divorce   2. Children of divorced parents
    I. Title
    306.8'9   HQ814
    ISBN   0-413-15030-5

To Ruhama, Benjamin, Rachel and David

Contents

Acknowledgements

If I were to list all the people who have influenced my life to the point of the writing of this book, it would begin to look like an autobiography! So I have chosen to mention just a very special few. They themselves know what they have meant to me: the late David Goldstein, Masha Goldstein, Aba and Frida Gefen, Karl Menninger, Lynn and Harvey Albert, Betty and Lloyd Macpherson.

Specific to the writing of this book, I would like to thank, for their assistance and encouragement: Matt Golan, Lucinda Vardey, Colleen Darragh, the lawyers, judges and above all the families who have trusted me to help them deal with their lives during separation and divorce.

Above all, I thank David Cravit, whose writing style and expertise in presenting ideas in a clear, concise fashion is manifested throughout this book. Working with him transcended the mere translation of thoughts into words, resulting in stimulating discussions which provided further thought and produced more ideas.

I am grateful to Margaret Robinson, Coordinator of the Conciliation Service at the Institute of Family Therapy, London, for adapting this book for its publication in the United Kingdom, and to Ann Mansbridge of Methuen for her help and advice in the preparation of this edition.

Finally, some people give you life, some nurture it, others support and alter it, while still others save it. There are those who give all of this and make life itself worth living. For this I acknowledge my wife and children.

Introduction

For most couples the decision to divorce does not come quickly or easily. The road to separation and divorce has probably been travelled in fits and starts, accompanied by heavy doses of anxiety and guilt. And the focal point for a lot of that guilt is the children.

'What about the kids?'

'I can't bear to hurt the children.'

'For the sake of the children . . .'

Around these genuine, loving, caring sentiments, there has grown up an entire mythology. A mythology that says children cannot survive a divorce without heavy, if not permanent, psychological damage. So some people stay in awful situations to 'protect' their children. Or if they feel divorce is absolutely unavoidable, then it must at least be 'packaged' so that the children are spared as many of the harsh realities as possible. Make promises to them. Avoid letting them confront their fears, real or imagined. Keep them happy. Lie to them, if they have to. Do anything . . . just as long as it keeps the kids from 'getting hurt'. So goes the myth.

The reality is quite different. As a psychiatrist involved primarily with child and family therapy, I have witnessed a great many divorces at close range. And my experience is that most children are quite capable of 'surviving' their parents' divorce with a minimum of psychological damage. They have reserves of emotional resiliency that adults rarely give them credit for. They can make it. They *can* survive.

Yet all too often they do not survive. They do get hurt. Sometimes very badly hurt – with effects that last for years and years, which in some cases can never be completely eliminated, even with treatment.

For a long time, I was both puzzled and frustrated by this. In case after case, I was able to satisfy myself that all the ingre-

dients were there to shepherd the children successfully through
the divorce with little or no long-term emotional damage. It
should have worked out fine.

From the parent, I almost invariably encountered love and
concern for the future of the children. Even in the most bitterly
contested divorce actions, even where the parents displayed the
most vicious behaviour towards each other, it was extremely
rare for me to find them indifferent toward the children's
future. On the contrary, they usually displayed strong feelings
of guilt about the effects of their marital battle on the children.
They wanted 'to do the right thing'. *Why, then, did they so often
fail?* From the child, I saw remarkable capacities to absorb
shock and bounce right back. *Why, then were the children so often
hurt?*

I began to realise that most parents do not understand how
relatively easy it is to help a child through a divorce. I saw
parents, who, in the throes of their own struggle, dealt with
their children in a destructive manner foreign to their natural
inclinations as parents. They were letting their own doubts and
fears and anxieties about the divorce intrude upon their natural
parenting relationship with their children.

*They were failing to realise that you can still be a father and mother,
without being a husband and wife.* This insight is deceptively simple. Yet it eluded most of the divorced couples whom I saw.
They assumed that their drastically changed relationship with
each other meant there also had to be a drastically changed
relationship with their children. So they stopped acting as
parents.

I was able to trace most problems back to this single issue.
And I was able to identify its main cause: an excessive concern
with the 'operational' problems of the divorce, the day-to-day
issues of logistics, lawyers, money, arrangements, that had
never been faced before, and that tended to obscure the fact
that a normal parenting relationship could, in fact, continue.

Mind you, it did not usually start off that way. At the
beginning, even as they were still reeling under the shock of
having finally decided to split up, most parents still thought
and acted as parents. They did not want their divorce to change
their relationship with their children. In the kinds of questions

they asked me – in the issues around which they sought my advice – they indicated all the typical 'parental' concerns.

But soon, that attitude was eclipsed by events, by what I have called the 'operational' problems of a divorce. These problems not only represented strange and new experiences, but very unpleasant and stressful ones, too: custody and property fights; dealing with the spouse's new girlfriend/boyfriend; logistical problems; financial worries; in-law pressures; social stigmas ... and many more.

And so the 'parental' state of mind that characterised the very early moments of the divorce situation became replaced, gradually but firmly, by an emotionally overloaded state of mind, in short by 'divorced' behaviour.

Meanwhile, of course, the children had not stopped needing their parents. True, the impending divorce may have imposed some unusual and even difficult physical or emotional constraints upon the parent–child relationship. But the child's need for that relationship, in whatever operational form, remained intact. It was not going to go away merely because the parents were now separated or divorced.

Nevertheless, as the parents continued to grapple with the problems and pressures of the divorce process, they continued to behave less and less like parents. Their sensitivities to their children's real needs tended to diminish. And so the children who, after all, could not suspend the process of growing up, increasingly went without having their real emotional needs met. This, far more than the changes in the physical or logistical arrangements of the household, became the root cause of long-term psychological damage.

In many cases, I had to undertake various psychotherapeutic procedures that addressed the specific problems and needs of the individual husbands, wives, and children I was treating. There was certainly no blanket cure for the problem. But in a surprisingly high number of cases, I was able to alleviate a great deal of the trauma with simple, common-sense recommendations to the parents on handling the everyday operational problems of the divorce so that they would *not* interfere with the normal process of being a parent. By showing them how to identify the child's real needs in the new situations the whole family was facing, by laying down some relatively straightforward 'do's' and 'don'ts', I was able to help many of my parents return to the business of parenting – and this in turn improved the odds that the children would come through it all with a minimum of emotional damage.

That is why I have written this book. My aim is to help parents going through a divorce to navigate the many strange new situations and pressures created by a divorce – *and still continue to be effective parents*. This book will tell you what to expect, what to be ready for. It will cover a wide variety of basic, day-in day-out problems and situations. I have drawn widely from my own patient files, and I will deal with children of all ages and divorces of all types.

While divorce laws vary from jurisdiction to jurisdiction, the basic sequence of events is usually fairly similar everywhere. In this book, I am assuming a four-step 'divorce process':

1. A decision to separate. The decision to make the separation permanent, through a divorce, may or may not be made at this stage.
2. A period of separation, with or without a formal legal separation agreement. During this stage, which may last from a few months to several years, there may or may not be negotiations leading to a divorce settlement. Dealings between the spouses may be amicable or hostile, and may be punctuated by frequent appearances in court.
3. The actual granting, by the courts, of a legal divorce. This stage includes the divorce hearings, judgements, appeals, and so forth.
4. The new life as divorced parents.

The above sequence should help you understand the situations and problems I will be dealing with in this book. It is *not* meant to serve as an accurate description of the legal steps you have to go through to get a divorce in your particular part of the world. It is very important for you to retain a lawyer, and nothing I say in this book should be interpreted as legal advice, or as a substitute for your lawyer's advice as to your legal rights, property rights, and best course of action through the legal system.

Two final but important points:

First, when I say it is not an overwhelming task to help your children come through your divorce with a minimum of long-term emotional damage, I am *not* saying the divorce itself is easy.

Your own reaction to your divorce may range from huge relief to mild inconvenience to massive trauma. A divorce is rarely completed without considerable emotional (and often physical) wear and tear. It usually takes hard work; it always demands patience and trust. But none of these things needs to disturb the fundamental parent–child relationship. While its framework may change, its inner integrity can remain untouched by even the most turbulent divorce.

Second, it is important to recognise – and be comfortable with – the fact that you are going to make mistakes. You will not always be able to follow every suggestion I make and have everything come out nicely and neatly. You will have 'off' days, there will be times when you misread your children's signals, moments when you simply make a mistake. *Don't worry about it.*

Think back to the way you reacted toward your parenting responsibilites before the divorce. You were probably fairly comfortable in knowing that you were not always going to be perfect in your handling of the children. Your divorce does not suddenly place upon you some special burden to be a 'Superparent', never to make a mistake.

This book makes only one assumption: that you are a committed, caring parent, and that you want to go on being that, despite your divorce. You *can* do it. I hope this book will show you how.

SOL GOLDSTEIN

CHAPTER 1

Breaking the News

This is how Chris Thompson found out his parents were getting a divorce.

He was six years old when it happened. He came home from school to find his father standing in the living room, a drink in his hand and a wild look in his eyes. At almost the same moment, he heard his mother let out a cry from the upstairs bedroom. Though no one had said a word yet, Chris became frightened and burst into tears.

His father grabbed him. 'Shut up!' his father screamed. Then: 'Don't cry. Be a man, now.' And finally, as Chris's tears began to subside: 'You're going to have to be a big boy from now on.'

Then his father let go of him and walked out of the house.

Shocked and bewildered, Chris ran upstairs to his mother. She was lying on her bed, her face buried in a pillow. When Chris came in, she sat up, grabbed him, and started to hug and kiss him.

Then she said, 'I'm all alone now.' Chris wondered what she meant.

She looked at Chris and said, 'Some day, you will leave me, too. You will leave me all alone, just like your father did.'

Still barely understanding what she was talking about, Chris instinctively reassured her: 'No, I won't leave you alone.' She squeezed his arm and said, 'Promise me. Promise me you'll never leave me alone.' So he promised.

Chris kept his promise to his mother. He continues to keep it to this day – almost thirty years later. He was never married. He still lives with his mother. He is an apparently successful executive, handsome, well-spoken, talented. But he has difficulty falling asleep at night. His appetite is irregular, and he confesses he sometimes finds it hard to get up in the morning. 'I know it sounds ridiculous,' he smiles apologetically to me, 'but sometimes I think there's really nothing to live for.'

Do all of Chris's problems go back to those first few moments, to the way in which he learned his parents were separating? Of course not. There is much more to it than that. The father was brutal, the mother was (and is) neurotic, and they were causing serious psychological damage to Chris long before they actually divorced. But what *is* true – and what concerns us here – is that those first troubled minutes, that terrible way in which Chris discovered the bad news, *set a pattern from which he was never to recover*. While it was by no means the only factor in his subsequent troubled life, the *method* by which his parents broke the news of their divorce *was* a factor, and an important one.

His parents never gave Chris a chance to deal with their divorce. His father just wanted to get out of the house. His mother just wanted to extract his promise of eternal attachment. Neither of them were interested in letting Chris express, and deal with, *his own* feelings.

Tina's parents never gave her a chance either – even though they broke the news to her with a lot more care and deliberation than did Chris's mother and father. They did it during a picnic. Tina still remembers what a wonderful day it was. Everyone was happy and smiling. Then, during lunch, Dad suddenly said he wanted to let Tina and her brother, Bobby, know about a little problem. Nothing serious, no big deal. But he was going to be moving out for a while. He and Mum thought it would be better if they lived apart . . . not that there was anything wrong, of course. Probably just for a little while.

Tina was stunned, but as soon as she started to ask questions, her father laughed and said, 'Come on, let's go and get some candy floss.' He gave her mother a great big kiss, and they both laughed and joked so hard that Tina had trouble figuring out why, if they were so happy now, they would want to live apart. But Bobby, she noticed, was saying nothing.

On the way home, both children were sullen. Tina wanted to be frightened but Dad was working very hard telling funny stories and her mother said she had never had so much fun in her whole life. Tina just did not know what to think.

Five years later, at seventeen, Tina sits in my office and sums it up perfectly: 'They never let me get upset. Not that day. Not the next day. Not ever. As soon as they thought a tear might be coming, they gave me candy floss.'

Here we have a situation very different from the horror show that Chris went through. Tina's parents seem, at first glance, thoughtful and considerate, doing anything in their power to spare their children undue pain. But although the package may be more attractive on the outside, it is every bit as lethal on the inside as it was with Chris. Today, Tina is a deeply troubled young lady, unable to express her emotions and intensely distrustful of relationships.

These two cases vividly demonstrate the kinds of problems parents can create for their children right from the outset, from the very moment of breaking the news of the divorce. By denying their children the two most vital needs – a sense of security and an opportunity to express their emotions – the parents rob the children of the strength to deal with what is to follow.

But before I talk about these two needs, what they mean, and how can you fulfil them, I want to deal with another important aspect of the two cases you have just read.

Both cases show the tendency of parents to think first of their *own* needs at this very intense and complicated moment. Focusing on themselves first, the parents cannot hope to instil the necessary emotional security in the children. Chris's father had a need just to get out of the house. Chris's mother had a need to secure her child's lifelong commitment to her. And Tina's parents, as we will see, had a need to convince themselves that their divorce really was not going to be as devasting for the children as the parents had feared.

Guess what? *All these adults' needs were met.* But the children's needs were not.

Don't think, by the way, that I am criticising the parents in these cases for *having* needs. All parents bring some very serious, and entirely legitimate, emotional or psychological needs into this situation. In fact, it is important to study what the typical parental needs are, so that you can better identify what your own particular package of needs might be.

What counts, though, is that you have to make sure you are not fulfilling *your* needs at the expense of your children's needs.

Let us consider those parental needs.

1. The Need To Explain the Decision

Parents often act out in front of their children the same debates and rationales that they present to other adults. A divorce is something that requires a lot of explaining – to friends, family, lawyers, judges ... and ultimately, to yourself. The urge to explain, to justify, to make a case, to prove a point, is perfectly understandable.

The arguments and explanations, however, are usually very complicated: complicated by the events that caused the split (other woman, other man, drinking, violence, etc.); complicated by the personalities of the participants (you, your spouse, hostile in-laws, meddling friends, co-workers, etc.); complicated by 'issues' (law, property, morality). Such complications can rarely be dealt with in a calm, reasoned way by *adults*, let alone by children. So as the parent starts explaining and re-explaining, the children suffer an immediate 'information overload', burdened with far more than they can comfortably handle. In many cases, I have seen parents simply overwhelm their children with forceful arguments about The Appropriateness Of This Step, The Rightness Of My Cause, The Reasons Why This Is Happening. Do *not* expect your children to wade through the circumstances that forced your split. You may be left with the self-satisfied assuredness that the children Understand My Point Of View – but what you really leave behind are confused and frightened little people, devasted by the event, and unable to make any sense of it in terms that are understandable.

2. The Need To Overcome Guilt

Most parents experience guilt feelings about the effect of their divorce on the children – and in many cases, they play out those feelings on the children themselves. We can see this quite clearly in Tina's case. By keeping Tina's tears away, her parents can reassure themselves that it really is not going to be so bad for Tina. Thus they relieve their feelings of guilt.

This guilt is easy to understand, and not to be condemned. A divorce does represent an enormous upheaval in the life of the child. For sympathetic, loving parents – and Tina's parents were – it can never be easy to witness such an upheaval.

So the parents ease their guilt by misleading their children about what is going to happen. They may delay breaking the news at all – and create that much more tension. They may, like Tina's parents, hedge and double-talk when the child asks specific questions. They may even deny what they have just announced! 'Things will work out great.' 'It'll probably be just for a while.' Parents seeking to relieve their own guilt almost invariably try to make light of the natural fears or insecurities that *must* strike children at this moment.

So the transaction ends with the parents fully convinced that they have built the necessary love and security into a difficult situation. See? It wasn't so bad. The children didn't even cry!

The parents are satisfied the divorce really is not going to be all that bad for the children after all. Therefore they, the parents, *have nothing to feel guilty about*. The parents now feel fine – which was the whole object of the exercise.

The children, on the other hand, feel more afraid than ever before, convinced that their anxieties must have been so terrible – and so well-founded – that their parents did not even want to acknowledge them. The children know full well that their parents have tried to con them, and in wondering why the parents would do such a thing, the children build up, within themselves, higher and higher levels of tension and insecurity. Clearly, if Mummy and Daddy had to lie about it like this, the future is going to be even more awful than first imagined.

3. The Need To Win the Children Over

This is a play that is acted out time and time again, particularly where the divorce is a hostile one, and particularly where that hostility derives from factors that may not have been apparent to the children (other man, other woman, financial problems, etc.).

The breaking of the news becomes a war of the gladiators, with the children expected to turn thumbs up or thumbs down when the dust finally settles.

So the problem and its solution – the decision to separate – gets presented strictly from the parents' point of view.

The presentation *technique* may vary from parent to parent – harsh, polished, sympathetic, clumsy – but this will only affect the degree of hurt to the children, and not the fact that *there will be hurt.*

I have seen that hurt display itself in my office . . . sometimes many years later. Children who blame themselves for having caused their parents' divorce. Or for not having been able to prevent it. Children who feel guilty about the way they responded to the pressures that were placed on them in that very first 'let's choose sides' meeting. They did choose sides, and they have questioned their choice and agonised over it ever since. Was it really Daddy's fault? Should I really have been so hard on Mummy? Did I turn thumbs down when my 'vote' should have gone the other way?

To an extent, these kinds of questions are very natural and will probably surface in the child's mind at some point in the divorce process. What is dangerous is letting these questions be raised as *part of the first step* – the moment of informing the child about the impending divorce. At that particular moment, the child is in no position to deal with these issues. To force them on the child can, at minimum, make the whole adjustment process much more difficult later on; at worst, it can cause irreparable harm.

4. The Need for Parents To Reassure Themselves

In this situation, there is only one actor in the drama – the individual parent.

The children might as well not be there at all, because what is happening is not a transfer of information, not a dialogue, but a soliloquy.

What this parent really wants and needs is to be able to recite the facts and the rationale of the divorce out loud, as a means of self-reassurance. See? I went over all the arguments one more time and they still make sense. See? The roof didn't fall in. See? I didn't get hit by lightning. It must be the right decision. I feel much better.

This kind of parent, in effect, talks to himself or herself, out loud, in front of the children. Any real information the children obtain is an accidental by-product of the parent's need for self-reassurance. The session ends with the parent indeed relieved, but the children confused and distraught.

In all four situations I have outlined, the parents are trying to deal with very real and legitimate needs of their own. These needs can, should and, indeed, *must* be met. In fact, a great deal of harm can be done by *never* considering your own needs, and *always* focusing on the children's needs at every step of the divorce process. It is wrong to deny your own adult needs, to postpone them, to shunt them to one side. Later in this book, I will tell you how to avoid becoming a complete prisoner of your children's equally real and legitimate needs.

But not now. Not at the moment of breaking the news to your children. The only adult need that has a place at this time is the need – indeed, the right – to maintain your integrity as a person, and, in addition, your *parenting* need to express your love to your children and your determination to go on being their parent. Otherwise, this moment belongs to them, and should focus on their needs first.

All children, regardless of their age, individual personality, or the circumstances within the family and surrounding the divorce, share the same two overriding needs in this situation: the need for security, and the need to express emotion.

Security can mean many different things to children, depending on their age, stage of development, family environment, and other facts. But in this situation, security means just one thing: the conviction that you will go on being their parents.

You may be fooled, however, when the children do not immediately express this particular definition of security but instead choose to focus on the physical or operational changes that are taking place. They may insist that what 'security' really means is that Daddy, in fact, does not move out! They may question, protest, even berate you for causing this upheaval in the structure of their lives.

But underneath all the questioning and probing, and possibly tears and pleas, what they are really looking for is some assurance that they can continue to rely on you for care and loving ... for parenting. **They must understand that even though the two of you will no longer be husband and wife, you can and will still be their mother and father**. You must convince them of this. It should be your single most important goal when you break the news of your divorce.

Expressing emotion is a basic human need, and it is essential to good mental health that this need be met. The need is particularly important at times of stress. If we are forced to bottle up our natural emotional responses to stressful events, we simply re-channel those responses into some other form, usually much more severe and damaging.

I'm not concerned, at this stage, with *the way in which* the emotions are expressed. One child will cry. Another will beg and plead, promise to do anything if only you will reconsider. Another will curse, accuse, even threaten. The specific responses of individual children depend on variables I will discuss below. What is important is that you realise your children have an absolute need to express their emotions, in whatever form, and that you must not interfere with this process. You *can*, through discussion, convince a child that you will go on being his parent. You *cannot* convince a child not to cry. Any suppressions of the child's natural expressions of emotion may do serious harm.

All children, as I said, have these two needs. But two factors determine how your child indicates his need for security, and his emotional needs: the child himself, and the home background.

Let's start with the child himself. Believe it or not, your divorce is not the only problem the child is facing right now! He is also confronting the *normal* developmental problems associated with his particular age. An infant who can comprehend little, but may sense a great deal ... a two-year-old in the throes of toilet training . . . an adolescent undergoing all the stresses of pre-adulthood: each of these children is experiencing particular emotional (and often, physical) stresses that are challenging enough to parents under the best of circumstances. And to some extent, the child's reaction to how you break the news of your divorce will be as much influenced by these normal growing-up pressures, as by the impact of the news itself and how you present it.

But of course, no two children are alike.

So, in addition to the 'textbook' growing-up influences associated with your child's particular stage of development, we also have the influences that derive from his unique identity and personality. This identity has no age limit. Is the child stubborn and independent? Shy and fearful? Quietly strong? Intelligent? Physically or emotionally self-confident? Openly loving? Gregarious? More attached to one parent than to the other? The leader of the children – or led by his siblings? All of these factors will influence what your child needs from you in this divorce situation; understanding your child's unique personality should also influence how you decide to inform the child of your divorce.

The second factor that comes into play in determining just how your child will respond to the news is the home background – the circumstances of the divorce itself, and of the home life that preceded the final break-up of the marriage. It is not difficult to see how different circumstances will dictate different scenarios for informing the children. Here are some actual cases I have been involved in.

- *The Armstrongs* are loving parents who have gradually watched their marriage come apart. Their deep concern for their children has prevented them from ever betraying even a hint of their marital problems. Both of them are 'together' people – there is no 'other woman' problem, no money problem, no hatred, not even mild dislike. They just simply do not want to be married any more. But they are determined to co-operate in making the divorce as painless as possible for the children. Both intend to be supportive of one another, and of the children, throughout the entire process. Both have read up on 'co-parenting' and intend to arrange joint custody of the children, and take equally active roles in the children's upbringing.

● *The McNaughtons* have been fighting for years, and their children are very suspicious – without having yet been told – that a parting of the ways is imminent. Each parent complains to the children about the other. Each wonders out loud what life would be like if only there weren't the burden of this terrible marriage. Yet both perceive in themselves a love for their children, and a genuine desire to spare the children from any hurt. Because of this, they have delayed and delayed the separation itself, let alone telling the children anything about it.

● *Mrs Mason* caught her husband with another woman, and instantly demanded a divorce. Mr Mason does not want a divorce, is contrite about his actions, and has been begging his wife to try to keep the marriage together. Not a hope. Mrs Mason, adamant, has already been to a lawyer. The children have no inkling of what is going on.

● *Mrs Stone* is in love with the tennis pro' – and the children know all about it. The older child, a thirteen-year-old girl, is not only mature enough to understand exactly what her mother is up to, but also has a pretty accurate idea of how things are going to unfold in the future. The youngster, a four-year-old girl, has only a vague perception of 'Uncle Bill'. So far, the older daughter has said nothing, protecting the mother. But Mr Stone's demanding career has triggered other problems in the marriage. When the inevitable break-up comes it will be initiated by Mrs Stone, and the news will come as no surprise to the older daughter, while it will shock and confuse the 'baby'.

● *The Hoffmans* have one of those marriages in which everything is wrong. He has had numerous affairs. She is an alcoholic, has undergone psychiatric hospitalisation, and is verbally abusive to the children. The Hoffmans have long since decided to split up, but each wants custody of the children, and each is in fighting trim.

Mr Hoffman has hired a lawyer with a reputation for being a 'gunslinger' in divorce actions; Mrs Hoffman's lawyer is almost as rough, tough and nasty. It promises to be a very ugly, and lengthy, battle for the kids. The children have picked up definite signals that something major is about to break, but they have not actually been told anything yet.

In each of these situations, the circumstances that led to the separation will, in and of themselves, exert a major influence on how the news is communicated to the children, and how they will respond. Shock, relief, fear, contempt for the parents, uncertainty, guilt – reactions such as these can often be traced directly to the reasons for the divorce itself, and how much the children already knew or sensed before being told.

We have seen, then, how the children themselves – their age, stage of development, and individual personality – and the home background can both influence how you choose to break the news of the divorce, and how the children may respond.

It is very important for you to pause and analyse both of these factors, as they apply to your particular situation, *before* you plunge right in and tell the children that your marriage is breaking up.

Start with the children. How old are they? At what stage of development are they? What problems are they having that could be considered 'normal' for this age? Focus in on these problems: do they provide clues as to how you should handle the situation?

Now consider your children's individual personalites, as distinct from the normal developmental influences of their age. What problems, strengths and weaknesses come to light?

Finally, take a hard-nosed look at the circumstances of your imminent divorce. Check some of the case histories above – does your situation come close to any of them? (Don't worry about matching every detail of the cases I have described.) Are the two of you agreeing to this divorce in the calm, almost amicable manner that the Armstrongs display? Or is one of you pushing a divorce that the other one doesn't want, like the Masons? Can you see yourself co-operating with your spouse in the post-separation period? Or is it to be an all-out war? *Why*

are you divorcing – and do the children already know, or
suspect?

Remember that even if the children do have some suspicions,
you are still going to be a little 'out of sync' with their knowledge and understanding of your marital problems. You have
probably been aware of the shaky state of your marriage for
some time – long before the children were. When you made the
decision to split up with your ex-, that decision probably came
at the *end* of a long process of argument, emotional upheaval
and possibly indecision. But for your children this news comes
as a *beginning*: of something new, of something perhaps startling
and unexpected, something frightening. They are at the starting point of a journey you have almost completed.

As you weigh up all these factors, try to anticipate how they
may affect that scene with your children, that first communication of the news. I am not suggesting that you literally write
out, word for word, what you are going to say. But by doing a
little thinking beforehand, you are at least focusing on the
situation and becoming more sensitive – if only instinctively –
to what it may call for. What is needed is a frame of mind,
rather than a hard-and-fast plan.

You have reminded yourself of the children's two overriding
needs: security (they need to be reassured that you are still their
parent), and the opportunity to express their emotions. Now
you are ready to tell them.

Here are some specific dos and don'ts.

1. Do it together

Except in extreme circumstances, the husband and wife
should be together when the children are told about the divorce. This in turn means you should develop a rough plan
together. Talk about what each of you is going to say; try to
anticipate what questions the children will ask, how to answer
them, which of you should answer which kind of question.
The plan can be flexible. You probably will not be able to cover every possibility, but you should at least be together on the
main issues. Regardless of how bitter or hostile the divorce action may be, this is a moment to put aside your own problems

and differences and communicate honestly and constructively with your spouse, so that the two of you may in turn communicate honestly and constructively, as parents, with your children.

2. Do it at home

Don't take the children for a special outing – a trip, the museum, the circus, a restaurant. We saw how Tina's parents did this, out of the mistaken belief that the shock and pain of the divorce would somehow get lost in all the hubbub and excitement. This is a serious mistake, and it is not playing fair with your children. Your divorce is *not* innocuous, and should not be presented to the children as if it were.

Choose a comfortable room, have all the children present, remove all distractions (TV, radio, toys, etc.) – and tell them.

3. Be honest

It is not easy to tell your children that your marriage is over. And it is even tougher to stick to your guns when the children start to cry . . . and perhaps even beg you to reconsider.

But you *must* stick to your guns, because what your children need more than anything is your complete honesty. Anything less erodes your credibility as a parent, and enhances the one great fear that is most critical to the child – the fear that you will somehow stop being his parent.

Lack of honesty is perhaps the most common mistake parents make in this situation. They want to spare the children the pain of facing what is going to happen. So they hedge. They may hold out some hope that it really will not happen at all, that the decision is somehow not really final. They may agree to reconsider, knowing full well that this is just a charade, and that the decision is irrevocable. Anything to stop the crying, to stop the pain of their children.

Yet this only causes more pain later on. It is unfair to the children to drag out that pain, prolong that hurt – especially to set up expectations that cannot be realised. In one or two cases I have seen, the parents allowed the children to 'persuade' them to reconsider, and the children were then emotionally battered by the ensuing period of tension as they waited for the second 'decision'. And when the original decision was upheld, as it inevitably had to be, the children blamed themselves and their conduct during the waiting period, and became chronically guilt-ridden. It sounds extreme but it can, and does, happen.

By all means, adapt your language, your style, your tone, and the amount of specific information you impart, to suit the age and maturity of the children. That is only common sense. But never compromise on honesty – the children need it, expect it, and are entitled to nothing less.

4. Allow the children to express their emotions

I have mentioned this before in a general sense, and I repeat it now because it is so critical. The children must have the emotional freedom to deal with this devastating news. Their reactions may take any of several forms:

- tears
- anger – either generalised ('I hate you; if you really loved me, you wouldn't do this.'), or specific (It's all your fault: if you were a better Mummy, this wouldn't have happened.')
- pleading – 'Please don't do this.'
- promises – 'If I behave better and always keep my room clean, will you please change your mind?'
- fear – 'What's going to happen to me?'
- intense rage – 'I want to kill you; I want to kill myself.'
- cynicism or false bravado – 'Big deal, who cares, what took you so long, I knew all the time, I don't care, I don't need you anyway.'
- denial – 'I don't want to hear about it.'

What do you do? Nothing. *Do not intervene.* Do not try to prevent the reaction from taking place. Do not admonish the child. And above all, do not, out of a mistaken form of sympathy for the child, attempt to talk him out of his particular form of emotional reaction. Such reassuring statements as, 'Don't cry, sweetheart, it won't be that bad, you'll see', only make it more difficult for the child to express the emotions, and the free expression of emotions is the best way for the child to gear up his system to deal with the situation he has now been presented with.

Remember, the child needs this moment of outpouring. It 'belongs' to him in a very real sense. Remember, too, that there is usually not much significance to the particular form of the expression of emotion, or to the particular words. When he says that he hates you, it does not mean that he really hates you. When he pretends to be cynical and uncaring, it does not mean that he really is cynical and uncaring. What these responses give the child is a release, a way of temporarily relieving the pressure. They are the necessary shock absorbers for the child's emotional system, helping him eventually achieve some measure of equilibrium in this very difficult situation.

It is dangerous for the emotions to remain pent-up inside. *Let them come out.* Then tell the child that you understand why he feels this way; that you know it really hurts; but that you will try to help him so that it will hurt less in time, and his feelings will change.

5. Be specific – but don't over-explain

Let the children know the details of future arrangements, if any of them have already been determined. Let them know the probable timing of events. When is Daddy moving out? When is Daddy coming to visit? The children are entitled to this information.

At the same time, it is important not to overwhelm the children – in particular, the youngest child – with too much information. A good rule of thumb is to let each child set the pace by asking the questions, instead of you rushing forward with a volley of information that the child may not be able to digest, and that may only get in the way of the child's expression of feelings. Always remember that for the child, this is a moment of feelings. The facts of the divorce can and should provide a context for those feelings, but not a jungle that tangles and inhibits them.

6. Don't ever attribute the marital problem to the children or involve them in the solution

Unless the children are very mature and have been witnesses to the marital problems that led to the divorce decision, I disapprove of telling the children that *anyone* is to 'blame' for the situation. To talk about 'Daddy's fault' or 'Mummy's fault' once again takes the play away from the children and stifles the free expression of their emotions.

But if the subject does come up, *never* lay the problems at the door of the children themselves. The point is an obvious one – in fact, very few parents ever do come right out and accuse the children of being responsible for their divorce. What many parents do, however, is involve the children in the *solution* to the marital problem, in the rationale for the divorce decision:

'We're doing it for your own good.'

'I honestly think you children will be happier if Daddy and Mummy don't live together any more.'

'If it turns out to be too hard for you, then I might think about coming back home.'

These kinds of statements make things much more difficult for the children. The statements do not reflect reality, and all they do is set up needless tensions, false expectations, and the seeds of future insecurities and anxieties.

7. Reassure the children that you will go on being their parents

The children see the divorce through their own eyes, and their main concern is, naturally, the impending 'loss' of a parent. They are almost certain to have, at best, only a very dim perception of the nuances of married life as the adult experiences it, so they cannot possibly be expected to identify with *your* feelings on the 'loss' of a spouse.

What they do know – without a doubt – is what it has meant to them to have you as their mother or father. And now you are going to be gone. Or your spouse is. Now they are hearing words they may never have heard before: separation, lawyers, custody, visiting rights. To the children, these words do not describe a broken *marriage*. They describe a broken *parenthood*.

Does your divorce mean the children will literally no longer have a mother, or a father? Of course not – *you* know that. You have to make the children know that too. They must be re-assured that you will still be available to them as parents. Regardless of the new living arrangements, the logistics, the timetables, the reasons why and why not, the children must understand that they will still be able to see you both, talk to you both, have you involved with their needs and problems just as you have been all along.

Tell them. Be specific. Relate it to concrete things you are now doing with them.

'Even though Mummy and I will no longer be living together as husband and wife, I will still be your Daddy. I'll still do all the things with you that we were doing before, like working with you on your skating and letting you come to the office on Saturday mornings.... '

'I'll be available to you. I'll help you.'

'Of course we'll finish up that project we were working on. And I've got some ideas for a few more.... '

You have three critical instructions to keep in mind as you break the news of your divorce to your children: be honest; be reassuring; be receptive to their emotions. And try to remember that breaking the news of your divorce can be both a problem and an opportunity. Its dimensions as a problem are easy enough to identify: getting the courage to say the words (and hoping you have found the right words); handling your guilt and uncertainty; having the strength to witness your children's expressions of shock, sorrow and even rage.

It may be less easy to understand how this terrible moment can also represent an opportunity. But it can. It can be an opportunity to equip your children to deal with all the other painful stages of the divorce, by building into their conscious-ness – right from the beginning – such a strong feeling of love and security, and such a conviction that the parenting rela-tionship you have with them will never be undermined, that none of the subsequent problems can ever truly overwhelm them.

If you show courage and honesty, your children will show courage and honesty, too – and you will both be well on your way towards successfully coping with whatever comes next.

CHAPTER 2

Separating

You have told your children the news. And almost immediately, if you are like most couples, you and your spouse physically separate. Often it happens that very day; rarely does it happen more than a few weeks later. So without much chance to learn about how your children are going to handle the situation, you are already in the thick of it – you are separated.

What now? What immediate problems can you expect? From your children? From your spouse? And even from yourself?

It's difficult to generalise about this transitional stage. Each divorce is very different, and reactions vary as much as the personalities involved. For the sake of convenience, then, I have established a few ground rules for this chapter.

What I call the 'separation stage' covers the entire period that *precedes* the handing down of the final divorce decree. But since this period can last for quite a long time – in some cases, for several years – in this chapter I am focusing on the *early stages*, during which the new arrangements and revised relationships are still not firmly established.

I am assuming that the separation is permanent, and will result in a divorce. It is not a 'trial separation'. This does not mean that there are no doubts and uncertainties, though. There are many – and I will be dealing with some of them in this chapter.

I have divided all separations into two main categories: peaceful separation, and non-peaceful separation. And I am assuming that one parent is leaving the home, the other remaining with the children. This assumption is to some extent arbitrary, since it excludes such situations as sharing the care and control, in which the child may move back and forth from one parent's home to the other's. It is also possible that the parent who remains with the children during the separation period may not wind up with custody of the children after the final divorce settlement. But even if your situation fits one of these exceptions, you should have little problem applying my advice accordingly.

Peaceful Separation

What I call a 'peaceful separation' has this main characteristic: the husband and wife, whatever their feelings towards each other (and these feelings can often be fairly hostile), are determined to work co-operatively when it comes to helping the children. They both want to go on being parents. This determination is sometimes thwarted by events, or by the basic emotional conflict that led to the breakdown of the marriage in the first place. 'Peaceful' separation does not mean that everything goes smoothly. But at least the initial motivation is there, to go on parenting.

Let's begin by looking at the feelings that each of the participants – outside parent, remaining parent, children – bring into the situation.

The outside parent's feelings are complicated by the physical separation from the rest of the household. Thus, while this parent shares many of the same questions and anxieties as the remaining parent, there is a different emphasis on issues of power and powerlessness. The remaining parent is, after all, in much more direct contact with the children. It is only natural for the other parent to wonder what will become of his or her effectiveness as a parent, and relationship with the children.

Here are the main issues, or questions, that are raised most often when I talk to the parent who has left the home. (Often it is the father.)

1. Will I be able to support them?
2. Will my ex-spouse allow me to be involved as a parent?
3. Will my ex-spouse be a good enough parent alone? Will I get enough input?
4. What if there's a school problem – will I be told about it? Will I get a chance to be involved?
5. What if the kids get sick? What if there's an accident – will someone be able to reach me in time?

These questions are all aspects of the same issue: since the physical relationship has changed, will the parenting relationship also change? The outside parent thus has the same worry as the children had when they first heard the news!

And this parent identifies, and inventories, all possible results of a change. One or two relate to pure circumstance: what if there's an accident and they can't reach me in time? But most concerns focus on the remaining parent's possible refusal to 'allow' the leaving parent to continue to be involved with the children.

It is important to understand that this fear exists in the mind of the outside parent, even when the two parents have already *agreed* to co-operate in raising the children. And this agreement, as I have pointed out, is usually one of the key features of a 'peaceful' separation. So what is the outside parent worried about?

This parent is *not* afraid of some formal, official refusal on the part of the remaining parent, a locking of the doors, ending of contact. Their prior agreement makes that unlikely in the extreme. The real danger, as this parent sees it and fears physically, is a subtle and gradual erosion of his or her parenting influence. This fear is in part based on a conscious, rational understanding of what *can* happen. But in large part, it is an emotional response, natural, normal, and in no way consciously disloyal to the remaining parent.

6. How much did I hurt the children by not being able to save the marriage?
7. How much will my leaving hurt them?
8. Will they blame me for leaving them?
9. Should I go back, for their sake?

These questions express a struggle that goes on within both parents, but particularly within the parent who is now physically separated from the children as well as from the spouse.

There is a profound tension between two conflicting emotions: relief that the marriage is over, and anxiety about the parenting relationship being over too. The break-up of an unhappy marriage was expected to bring relief. Instead, it brings feelings of guilt, isolation, loneliness. Some of these feelings, it is true, do not relate to the children: there are problems of being 'single' again, going out, finding relationships with the opposite sex. The solution to such problems is often difficult, and contributes to these feelings of loneliness or isolation. But the feelings are made all the more acute by the physical separation from the children.

The absentee parent, alone and brooding, not experiencing the relief that was to be expected from the separation, now has the time and the emotional inclination to focus in on the broken physical relationship with the children. And it is easy, then, to conclude that this physical separation *must* somehow wind up being harmful to the children. Which only increases the guilt.

Now the absentee parent is no longer worried simply about the ex-mate's power to damage the relationship with the children. In this new series of questions, this parent wonders if his or her relationship with the children is *inherently* impaired. Impaired – quite apart from what the remaining parent does – by the simple act of *leaving*. So the nagging thought is, 'It must be my fault.'

To avoid exploring this disturbing issue too much, the outside parent often rushes into a new relationship with someone else which, if it does not solve the problem of separation from the children, at least provides a distraction. It can also be seen as having a side benefit: the creation of 'a more home-like atmosphere for the kids' at that parent's new residence. Sometimes, this parent will be so overcome with guilt that he or she will run back into the marriage, and move back home. This solves the tension about the children, but re-creates the unhappiness that caused the marriage to founder in the first place. In most such cases, the returning spouse will soon provoke a fight to 'prove' that the original decision to separate was the correct one.

10. What do I do with my new 'freedom'?
11. What kind of lawyer will my ex-spouse hire? What kind of lawyer should I retain? Will I be able to protect myself?
12. What do I tell my friends/family/co-workers? How do I face them?
13. Am I a 'loser' for having a broken marriage? Am I a heel for having left the home?

This last group of questions simply shows that, in addition to the parent–child relationship and the problems it causes in the mind of the outside parent, there are also several strictly *adult* concerns that are important at this time. They usually occur in the mind of a childless person, too. They are perfectly natural and normal in this situation.

Accept these feelings. *Recognise* that they result from your new situation. *Recognise* that, with time, these feelings will diminish. And *refrain* from taking on your entire future life all at one time. You do not have to satisfy these concerns immediately. Deal with things one day at a time. There is no single sudden 'answer' that will make your feelings and concerns go away. Be aware of this, and try to be relaxed about it.

The *remaining parent* obviously does not face the kind of insecurity caused by physical separation from the children. If nothing else, this parent enjoys constant contact with the children, and the opportunity to carry on the parenting relationship that existed before the separation.

But this seeming advantage is a two-sided coin, for it means the remaining parent is also much more intensively exposed to the children's emotional response. Not infrequently, for example, the children will make accusations against both parents, but the brunt of these is borne by the parent who is still in the house.

This kind of pressure can make it difficult to be an effective parent, and there are many ups and downs and apparent 'failures' to deal properly with the children. Such failures can erode the self-esteem of the parent, who is often already feeling deep insecurities about the failure of the marriage and his or her desirability as a spouse.

Basically, there are three major emotional struggles going on inside the parent who has remained with the children:

1. Loss of self-esteem

When the marriage breaks up, both parties feel somewhat insecure about their worth as a partner in a relationship. We saw how the outside parent can indulge in self-accusation: 'Am I a loser? Am I a heel for having left?'

This same emotion becomes wider and deeper for the parent who has stayed in the home. Since the children are right there, ever-present reminders of yet another relationship that could be lost, the remaining parent goes on to wonder: 'If I'm not good enough to hang on to a spouse, maybe I'm not good enough to hang on to my children either. What's wrong with me, anyhow?'

2. Feelings of loss and abandonment

This is a basic human fear that we acquire in infancy and, to some extent, never entirely lose. Now the fear has been realised. For some people, the separation evokes the same emotional response as the death of a loved one. There is a sense of bereavement, grief ... even despair. This is an emotional response that often has nothing whatsoever to do with the conscious, rational opinion of the departing spouse: the sense of bereavement can be present even where the relationship was extemely hostile, and the departing spouse an object of disdain. Of course, the feeling will not take the same outward form as grieving for the death of a loved one. Typical responses will include running quickly into a new relationship; fighting with the ex-spouse (especially over the children) in order to provide a reason *not* to feel grief; or, conversely, attempting a reconciliation.

3. Feelings of confusion with regard to the children

Just as the departing spouse thought about the new 'freedom', so does the remaining spouse. But the freedom may be severely curtailed by parental responsibilities ... responsibilites which affect the remaining parent far more than the outside parent. So, on the one hand, you may feel 'saddled' with the children, resentful of their demands and their incursions on the new freedom. On the other hand, you may desperately need the children to replace the loss of your spouse. So there is confusion and, often, considerable emotional turmoil.

These three major struggles emerge in a variety of questions and expressions of feelings, ranging from strictly pragmatic topics to issues that deal with emotional security. Here are some of the questions I often encounter with parents who have remained in the home with the children.

How will I manage alone with the children?
What if they get ill? What if there are school problems?
How do I handle the questions the children may ask me about the divorce? About something my ex-spouse has said to them? About what's going to happen in the future?
How do I handle their feelings?
What kind of support can I count on from my ex-spouse? Financially? Practically? Emotionally?
Will I have to get a job outside the home?
If I do, how will I handle both my job and the raising of the children?
How do I handle all my kids' activities? Dropping them off somewhere? Picking them up? Can I get them everywhere they have to go, and keep them on schedule?
What kind of lawyer should I look for? The peacemaking type? Or should I listen to everyone who's telling me to find a real fighter?
How do I explain all this to my friends/family/co-workers? What if they offer me money, or help?
Why was I left? What's wrong with me? Will I be able to live without my ex-spouse? Will anyone else love me?
Will my children blame me for 'kicking out' their other parent?
Will my children look down on me and not respect me because I'm the one that was left? Does it make me less of a person?

As you can see from these questions, the remaining parent has many of the same concerns as the other parent. They are, however, extended or broadened by the continued physical contact with the children. What to the outside parent was a vague, 'Can I still be an effective parent?' becomes, to the remaining parent, a host of very specific fears about organisation, logisitics, money, 'arrangements' – the business side, if you will, of parenting, the burden of which falls mainly on this parent.

The *children*, perhaps not surprisingly, have the widest range of concerns, and the list of their questions can seem like a confused jumble of the very profound and the very mundane. There are

intense emotions: fear, guilt, rage. There are far-reaching
issues, even if they are not always accurately articulated. What
will happen to the family? How will this affect me later on? And
there are a host of everyday, down-to-earth problems: what to
tell friends, how to get to piano lessons. But everything derives
from one central issue: *will I still have parents*?

These are some of the questions you will hear, or emotional
responses you will see, in your children:

1. What happened? Why? Why did it happen to me?
2. What did I do that caused this? Maybe I was too
demanding? Maybe I misbehaved too much? Would it have
been different if I had followed all the rules that my parents
set down?
3. I'm angry at my father for leaving. But I still want to see
him. Does he still love me? Does he still want to see me?
4. I'm also angry at my mother because, after all, she threw
my father out. But if I say how I feel, will I be thrown out too?
5. Will my brother and sister and I stay together, or will we be
divided up just like the sofa and stereo and paintings were
divided up? And if that happens, where would I end up? With
Mummy? Or with Daddy? And how do I feel about that?
6. Will we still live in this same house? Can I still have all my
friends over to play?
7. What if my friends find out about this? Will they still like
me? Will they tease me? Maybe I should tell them first – but
how?
8. Should I tell my teachers? Or will Mummy and Daddy do
that? Should I ask them about it? Or wait and see what
happens?
9. Will I still go to the same school? Or will Mummy and
Daddy make me change schools so my old teachers won't find
out about this?
10. Who's going to take me to piano/football/ballet?
11. Who's going to cook for us? Get us ready for school? Mow
the lawn? Shovel the snow? Can one parent do all that alone?
12. Will *I* have to become Daddy around here?
13. And if I *do* become the Daddy, and don't do a good job,
does that mean I'll get kicked out too?
14. Can I get Mummy and Daddy to be friendly again?

15. (Most often with adolescents, not with younger children) Who do they think they are, trying to tell me what to do? They've behaved like kids themselves. They're certainly not as wonderful as they think they are, if they could pull a stunt like this!

You should not be surprised to see the degree to which your children focus on themselves, and on the effect of the divorce on their lives, not yours. Older children may sometimes wonder out loud what went wrong with the marriage, and may ask point-blank, 'Are you going to be going out with someone else now? Can I meet Dad's new girlfriend?', but the divorce as a marriage breakdown (as opposed to *parenting* breakdown) is almost never the prime concern.

From the lists of questions, or issues, that affect the outside parent, the remaining parent, and the children, we can see that there is a host of emotions swirling around inside all three participants, and all of it coming at a time of maximum instability and uncertainty. The separation is just under way, and no one is quite sure what is going to happen.

Is there something you should actively *do*? Is there some timetable you should set for yourself, some 'result' that you must obtain vis-à-vis your children within a certain period of time? Or should you be patient and just let nature take its course, let the new arrangements unfold and let everybody get comfortable with them? Should you hope that, gradually, there will emerge some new sense of security within the children?

In terms of broad strategy, you should definitely follow this second option. Your children's very natural doubts and fears cannot be resolved quickly. While it is certainly important for you to *tell* your children that the parenting relationship will continue, they will not be completely secure until they can see for themselves the truth of your words. And this must take time. It cannot be forced in a few minutes – or even weeks. The children must grow into a feeling of comfort with the new situation – they cannot be pushed.

So the separation period is one that requires your patience – at a time, admittedly, of emotional upheaval for you. You must deal with your children's feelings, and not be overwhelmed by them, or run away from them. Yet you must also have the toughness *not* to try to solve everything all at once – the discipline to understand that the process will be slow, and the knowledge that it could be painful. There are no short cuts.

Your children's feelings should be dealt with as rationally as possible: there is no need for you to indulge in amateur psychiatry. Understanding the source of the children's most typical concerns, you should be able to handle most situations. Where there are severe problems, do not hesitate to seek professional help.

When I say that the separation period is one of patience, of letting nature take its course, of just plain *being a parent* and letting the children discover that your parenting can, and does, continue, I am not denying that there will be situations that *do* require a particular kind of action or response. There are things you can do to make the whole process easier; there are things you should definitely not do. Let's review them.

DON'TS

1. Don't talk to your children about a reconciliation. (Remember my earlier assumption that we are dealing with a real separation that will lead to a divorce, and not a 'trial separation'. Both you and the children must face the reality of the separation and impending divorce. False hopes only complicate things, and set up more extreme problems later on.
2. If the children ask you about a reconciliation, don't tell them that you are ready to try, but that the other parent is not (even if that is true).
3. Don't encourage the children to act as matchmaker or reconciliator with your ex-spouse.
4. Don't blame the other parent for what happened. Don't blame the other parent's family or friends.
5. Don't blame the children for having caused all of this by their (mis)behaviour. Yes, I know, you would never set out deliberately to make that kind of accusation. But there will be moments when you are exasperated by their current misbehaviour, and perhaps tense and upset by some problem with your ex-spouse, and you may just lash out: 'Maybe if you'd behaved a little better than you're behaving now, all of

this wouldn't have happened.' Be careful – watch what you say! You cannot take the words back, and they can do a lot of harm to the children.

6. Don't blame yourself either. This can set up a mood of self-pity and anxiety that the children can quickly detect. It often leads to a role reversal, in which the children end up parenting *you*!

7. Don't tell the children not to talk about the other parent, and about their feelings of missing him or her. You may interpret such feelings as being a reflection on you ('How can they really love me when they still miss *him*, that no-good-so-and-so!'), but your ex-spouse is still their parent – and will be forever – and they are entitled to their feelings, and to the natural expression of those feelings.

8. Don't tell the children not to cry, or nag, or fight, or behave in any way that bothers you *when the reason it bothers you is not the behaviour itself*, but everything else that is happening to you. It is not fair to the children to impose your problems on every moment of their time including their normal, natural behaviour. (You are not superhuman, though, and it can be difficult to put up with the ordinary day-to-day rumpus – and I'll have some suggestions for this in the 'Do's'.)

9. Don't tell the children to leave you alone and not burden you with their problems because you are so overwhelmed. Remember that they are still going to have their normal complement of child-level problems that have nothing to do with the divorce. They need your response as their parent. The fact that those problems may seem trivial, compared to your divorce, is immaterial.

10. Don't tell the children not to worry about a thing because you or your ex-spouse will take care of everything. I am not suggesting you share with them every single problem or uncertainty that faces the household. But don't offer vague, blanket reassurances either. After all, they had previously placed their trust in their parents' staying together and living happily ever after . . . and look what happened. If you now tell them that everything is going to be fine, and it is *not* fine (as of course it *won't* be, sometimes), this will further undermine their trust in you.

Enough 'Don'ts'? Now let's look at what you can *do*.

DO's

1. Do allow for the direct expression of your children's feelings.

2. Do allow your children to yell at you and tell you they hate you for having allowed, or forced, their other parent to leave. This is a normal, natural emotion that must not be suppressed. Your response, however, must not be just to listen and then walk away, hoping that the storm has blown over. Tell them that you understand this is how they feel. If your Mummy and Daddy had split up, you would have felt the same way. But you still love them very much, and you know their other parent also still loves them very much. Even though they are angry with you, and hurt by you, you're sure that they still love you too, and because of that, you'll all be able to deal with this terrible thing in a less painful way, and after a while it won't hurt so much. *This line of argument is, in a sense, your response to all emotional upheavals that will occur with your children. It is so important that you may have to re-state it a thousand times during the next few months.*

3. Do allow them to tell you that they want to live with the other parent, without your dissolving into tears or having an acute anxiety attack. But tell them that you and their other parent will be working things out so that they can have time with each parent and will suffer as little as possible from the separation.

4. When you can clearly identify a request that is deliberately meant to hurt you, and to play you off against your ex-spouse, point this out to the children, and if circumstances permit, tell your ex-spouse, so that you can both co-operate in stopping this from becoming a destructive tool of a hurt child.

For example, your child may ask you to buy him something to which he knows he really is not entitled and, more importantly, that you cannot afford. 'If you don't buy this for me, I'll get Daddy to.' Tell the child you understand he is making this request because he feels badly. You're not going to respond to the request because it isn't the right thing to do

(explain why), and you know this may make the child feel
even more angry. But you still love him very much, and you're
sure that he loves you, even if he's angry with you. This is the
same line of argument outlined in point 2, above. You cannot
say it often enough.

5. Do insist on as little disruption as possible in the normal
household routine. Let the children keep the same household
chores, be governed by the same TV schedule, homework
time, same rules and regulations. Don't try to make this a
'happy time' by doing things to help them forget – they cannot
forget that you are separated . . . but they can learn to handle
it. One way to deal with it is to see that it does not change
every single aspect of what their life was like before their
parents split up. So 'special events', like trips to restaurants,
movies, etc., should happen only as often as before.

6. When your young child returns to the bottle, or thumb-
sucking, or wetting the bed, or not sleeping, or begins to
chew nails or stutter, *don't panic* but *do be aware* that the
child is expressing personal difficulties with the situation
through what is called regressive behaviour. While not all
children display this behaviour, it happens very frequently,
and it is therefore something you should understand, and
watch for.

Regressive behaviour is a symptom of the tension the child
feels as a result of your separation. The expression of this
tension is somehow stifled, and takes the form of regressing.

In simple terms, you can deal with regressive behaviour by
letting the child know, *at a level the child can understand*, that you
are aware of the tension being felt and that it would be better
to express these feelings directly to you, in words, or even in
crying, than to be hurt *personally* by indulging in this regressive
behaviour. Don't humiliate or blame the child for this
regression. Simply encourage your child to choose another
way of expressing personal feelings.

Be sure to communicate what is happening, and how you
have handled it, to the other parent. Both of you should
repeat, as often as possible, the key statement in point 2,
above.

That is the simple explanation, and general strategy, for

dealing with regressive behaviour. But your situation will depend a great deal on the age of the child – both in terms of what he does and how you should respond – so it is important that we look at this issue in somewhat more detail.

Usually, a child will regress to an earlier form of behaviour, characteristic of an earlier phase of development:

- a child who has just been toilet trained will begin to have 'accidents' again;
- a child who has just learned to speak will revert to baby talk;
- a child who has just learned to read regresses in schoolwork;
- a child who has shown some independence, now clings and whines, cannot sleep alone, becomes much more demanding;
- a child's play pattern may become disrupted – the child may claim to be bored and have no joy in activity; or may suddenly become hyperactive and aggressive, engaging in destructive forms of play;
- older children may cease to co-operate, fight more, engage in much more teasing or other forms of provocative behaviour with their brothers and sisters;
- teenagers may regress in schoolwork, make drastic changes in their relationships (new friends, new gangs), may not want to be around the house, may become uncharacteristically rebellious. It is not unusual to encounter drug experimenting, truancy, and other severe discipline problems;
- there is diet disruption at all ages – the child may play with food, stop eating, overeat;
- a very important category is the pseudo-mature child, dangerous in that we may be lulled into a false sense of security by the child's exaggerated 'goodness' and 'maturity'. This child is actually avoiding all issues, by being 'extra good', non-demanding, emotionally calm, trying to look after the parent. While technically this may not be a step backward in behaviour, the problem deserves to be categorised here because *the child is not behaving*

naturally. The solution usually lies with a careful check, by
the parent, of his or her own behaviour. Typically, the
parent has become too self-involved; the child sees that the
parent is sad, depressed, withdrawn, aloof – not available.
The child feels guilty and threatened – if the child intrudes
or disturbs the parent, the parent may be lost altogether. So
the child gives up personal needs to serve the parent's. This
is not a healthy resolution of the problem, and it needs
attention. Treat this in the same way as you would treat the
other indications of regressive behaviour.

These are some of the more frequent forms of regressive behaviour. In dealing with them, do not forget to consult the other
parent; keep each other abreast of your progress, what you are
saying to the child, what response you are getting, what
changes have been accomplished in the child's behaviour.

Time, and effective communications with the child, will help
these symptoms gradually disappear. If they do not, or if they
appear to be getting worse, consult your family doctor. Your
lawyer may also have some experience with this kind of problem, and may be able to refer you to appropriate professional
help.

You may also know other parents who have gone through
similar problems, and their advice (or just plain moral support)
may be helpful. Be careful *not* to listen to potentially destructive
advice from an embittered survivor of a strongly contested,
vindictive divorce. Know to whom you are talking, before you
ask for advice.

I have said that effective communication with the child is a
key to eliminating regressive behaviour. The child needs to
channel his feelings – his tensions – into other forms of expression. One way of providing this opportunity is to have regular
family meetings. Such meetings provide a forum in which you
can all share your problems: your fears, sorrows, frustrations
and even angers. They should be regularly scheduled. Everyone should be given a chance to talk – the children first, and
then you. The children will automatically become better listen-
ers if they are allowed to express their feelings or ideas first.

7. In addition to regressive behaviour, which is basically an

on-going pattern of conduct, you should also be ready for shorter-term or even 'one-off' incidents of extreme behaviour or reaction: isolated truancy, temper tantrums, fights, stealing, the occasional nightmare, or psychosomatic problems such as stomach-aches, headaches and related ailments.

Studies have shown that when there are no issues involving the children during the parents' divorce, the children will usually return to normal behaviour and normal development within one year of the separation. The reaction of adolescents, in particular, quite often becomes one of helping the younger children in the family and being extremely empathetic toward the parents. It is important and healthy for the children to help each other out, and give each other emotional support – but be careful not to encourage the children to take on the role of the 'missing' parent.

8. All of these situations have to be dealt with at a time when your own needs and feelings may be in a turmoil. Recognise this – and try not to feel guilty about apparent conflicts between your needs and your children's needs. Naturally, you want to give your children love and security. But you may at times rebel at having to pour so much emotional energy into your children – at the expense of your own legitimate needs and feelings. The process can be exhausting. There will be many moments when you want to cry out, 'What about *me?*' This is a natural reaction, and nothing to feel uncomfortable about. Later in this book, I will show you how to ensure that your own needs do not always take second place.

Non-Peaceful Separation

In a non-peaceful separation, the husband and wife do *not* work co-operatively when it comes to helping the children. The extreme conflict that existed during the marriage continues into the separation period, and often it centres around the custody of, or access to, the children. So, by rights, this kind of separation should be much more difficult to deal with than a peaceful (or co-operative) one.

But everything has its good side, as well as its bad side. And the one thing you have going for you, in this separation, is that precisely because the problems of the marriage were so visible, the shock of separation is probably not as great. Not to you, and not to the children either. They have seen it coming. They are ready for separation. They may even be relieved.

In many cases, family life will actually *improve*. Adolescents, for example, will often volubly condemn both parents for not having separated sooner . . . . and then pitch in and help the remaining parent take care of younger children.

Before I paint too rosy a picture, however, let me emphasise that this lack of shock or surprise on the part of the children reduces or eliminates only one of the problems you can expect to face during a separation period. You are still left with a host of other difficulties – and now with an unco-operative spouse.

Your first problem is that your children may have had a good relationship with that unco-operative spouse! While they can understand perfectly well why *your* relationship with him or her should be finished, they still want *their* relationship with your ex- to continue. This is true in the majority of cases I have handled. The children were able to see how terrible the parents' marriage was; they were able to understand the logic of the separation; it came as no surprise to them. But a terrible spouse might still have been a good parent – or, at the minimum, a parent whom the children loved, even if they were not always quite sure why.

The children wanted to keep on seeing both parents, even though each parent could not stand the sight of the other. So the children wound up with very mixed feelings: identifying with one parent whom they loved meant they were identifying with a person who caused anger and perhaps even hatred on the part of the other parent (whom they also loved).

In situations like this, there is bound to be a great deal of conflict and pain. How do you deal with it?

1. Don't condemn the other parent in front of your children.
2. Do feel free to acknowledge your own feelings towards the other parent, but separate those feelings from the children's feelings. You can say that Mum/Dad has been bad to you and that you don't like her/him any more, *but* you know this parent has been good to the children, and you don't blame the children for wanting to be with the other parent some of the time.

Studies have shown that even when children have been
mistreated by their parents, they can still remain quite loyal to
them and want to continue a relationship with them. These
children tend to blame themselves for being 'bad', and thus
deserving of the abuse. Such guilt feelings will vary, of course,
depending on the age and personality of the individual child,
and they are problems that require professional help.

Having reassured the children that you can understand
their feelings toward the other parent, you are still left with a
problem: your own feelings about having them visit that other
parent. These feelings can be particularly acute if complicated
by a custody or access battle. For the moment, I will assume
that your arrangement allows the other parent access to the
children, even though you may be working to change this
situation.

3. Don't tell the children they should not, or may not, visit the
other parent, because *you* think it's *bad for them*. Review, in
your own mind, your reasons for opposing or prohibiting a
visit. Does it really have anything to do with what is best for
the *children*, with your ex-spouse's abilities or deficiencies as a
parent? Or could it be that you really want to punish your ex-
for your past and present conflicts?

4. Do recognise that the other parent may have behaved badly
because of stress within the marriage, but now, freed from that
stress, may actually behave in a much more constructive way
towards the children. You have to be mature enough, in this
situation, to put your feelings to one side and try to be objective about what really is happening between your ex-spouse
and the children. In many families, I have seen marked
differences between the behaviour of the husband and wife
towards each other (vicious) and the behaviour of each one
of them towards the children (caring and sensitive).

5. Be patient. Allow the children and the other parent to work
on the new relationship.

6. Stay on the lookout for signs that your children are suffering
as a result of contact with the other parent. (But be honest
with yourself – is the problem *really* caused by the contact with
the other parent, or is the true cause your own reaction to this
contact?) If you think there is a problem, contact your lawyer

or family doctor to arrange for a professional assessment of what is happening, and whether or not this contact with the other parent should continue. If you are the parent who has remained in the house with the children, the 'contact' obviously means visits with the parent who has left. If you are the parent who has left, then the 'contact' means custody itself. Either way, if you are in one of those rare situations in which the other parent is actually harming the children's physical or mental health, you must do all within your power (and the court's) to restrict, or even prevent, all contact with that other parent.

7. If no harm is being caused, however, allow the children the maximum amount of freedom to enjoy their contact with the other parent, and to tell you about that enjoyment. It *can* be difficult to tolerate. The other parent may be behaving terribly towards you, but beautifully towards the children. You may feel very lonely every time the children are away. If you are the parent who has remained in the home with them, it can be particularly difficult to prepare them for the visit to the other parent, to watch their excitement, watch them go out and 'have fun', while you are stuck with their schoolwork problems, the day-to-day discipline, baths, brushing teeth, all the mundane 'chores' of being a parent.

You are entitled to feel unhappy! But recognise that this is *your* problem, not the children's problem. In some cases, I have seen children noticing the remaining parent's depression at their leaving, and then hesitating to go with the other parent. As soon as they get out of the house, though, they are fine. But the conflict can be intense – 'If I go with Daddy, I'll have fun and make Daddy happy; but if I go with Daddy, I'll also make Mummy very unhappy.' This conflict can emerge in a variety of ways, including the regressive behaviour I outlined earlier in this chapter.

8. Do not use the children's visits to the other parent as a leverage point in your divorce settlement negotiations. The worst damage I have seen done to children has occurred when parents use visitation to manoeuvre better settlements of property rights, maintenance, support payments, etc. These issues should be completely separate from anything else –

especially anything concerning the children. Don't manipulate your ex-'s access in order to further *your* cause in the
divorce negotiations. You may hurt your spouse – which is
probably exactly what you want to do – but if *that* is what you
want, why not use your fist, instead of your children. (Of
course I would not recommend either!)

When the marriage has been rough, and there is now a battle
going on in the courts, you have to face up to some very
searching questions. Perhaps the most important one is this: is
your 'plan of battle' really serving another purpose? Is it really
somehow a *continuation* of the marital relationship? A lot of my
clients are taken aback when I make this point to them. 'You're
not really engaged in divorce – you're engaged in an on-going
relationship which has merely taken another form. You're
separated, but you're still fighting.'

Divorce should be just that – final separation. The only
continuation of the relationship is around the children, since
both of you remain their parents for life. Other than working
out that relationship, why continue the battle?

Each time you struggle with your ex-spouse, look at it carefully:

• Is there a real issue at stake, something really worth
  fighting for? (There may well be – you may have to keep
  fighting to protect yourself, your property rights, etc. Just
  make sure that is really what it is all about!)
• Is the struggle worthwhile?
• Could there even be some enjoyment you are deriving from
  the struggle? Do you like making your ex- squirm?

And then ask yourself:

'To whom am I really doing this? My ex-? Or the children?'

I have yet to hear any parent – even those involved in the
most vitriolic court battles – say anything *other* than: 'I'd do
anything for those kids; I'd lay down my life for those kids.' Yet,
having said those words, back they go for another day in court,
ready to do possibly irreparable harm to their children over
some relatively minor issue. *Examine your real motives for doing
battle.*

Now let's say you have done exactly that. You have taken a hard and honest look at your feelings, your real motives, and you have concluded that you really do have a problem. The person on the other side really *is* being unco-operative, really is forcing you into a battle that you think has to be fought, even though the children may get tangled up in it. What do you do now? What *don't* you do now?

There are several different things you can try.

1. *Start by cooling the temperature.* The other person is often being unco-operative as a defence against (what he or she sees as) similar attitudes coming from you. Make sure, then, that you yourself are communicating a sense of co-operation. The chances are the other side will begin to relax, too.

2. *Instruct a responsible lawyer.* In most towns you will find lawyers who place fair settlement *ahead* of victory in a court battle. Try to find such a lawyer. If you need information or advice, contact the Solicitors' Family Law Association, or the Law Society in your particular district, and ask them to suggest a few names.

There are also lawyers who see themselves as 'hired guns', who are out to get the best deal *at any cost*. It may be tempting to instruct one of them – there is a natural urge to wreak vengeance on someone who has caused you so much misery in your marriage. But the real victim will be you … and your children.

I have seen many cases in which two tough lawyers continued their struggle to the point where their clients were actually forgotten, irrelevant, helpless participants being pushed further and further apart. On the other hand, I have been fortunate enough to see even more cases in which two reasonable lawyers have sat down and negotiated constructively, for the benefit of their respective clients. They have ended up with settlements which were fair, effective, prompt, practical and beneficial to everyone. Even serious confrontations and major differences have been settled in this atmosphere of co-operation.

Do not be concerned that co-operation will somehow force you back into the unwanted marriage. Believe it or not, I have

seen many fights continue because the two parties were
actually afraid that co-operation would somehow lead to
reconciliation! It *won't* happen. What will happen is that you
will arrive at a condition of stability and security – a situation
in which the thorny issues are settled, and in which both of
you can continue your parenting relationship with your
children in a peaceful atmosphere.

3. *Don't let anyone else make your decisions*. In particular, don't
allow yourself to be influenced by all the friends, relatives and
so-called well-wishers, who are working out their own marital
frustrations vicariously, through encouraging you to 'fight for
your rights'. No, I am not trying to demean your friends and
family, many of whom are bound to be quite sincere. But I
have seen too many cases in which interference from the side
lines prolonged and intensified something that could have
been cleaned up much more quickly, and with much less pain.
Trust your own judgement. Weigh up all the factors as carefully as
possible, thinking of how they affect *your children and you*, and
not how they are going to look to the spectators egging you on.

4. *If you have to, pay the heavy tax*. Nobody likes to pay more for
food, heat, utilities, clothing. But we know they are necessities
of life, so we find ways to adjust to higher costs.

It is the same in this situation. Your necessities are a resolution of the problem, and a peaceful atmosphere in which to go
on parenting your children. To obtain these necessities, you
may have to give in and let the other side have a 'victory'. You
may have to meet your ex-spouse much more than halfway.

Remember that I am not trying to advise you on the
specifics of your property settlement, maintenance needs, etc.
By all means be guided by your lawyer! What I *am* asking you
to recognise, though, is the 'bottom line': at some point, you
have to decide to *buy* those necessities. For example, when it
comes to valuing and dividing up property, you may have to
stop short of fighting for every last penny, and concede a
hundred pounds or so to your ex-spouse. The money you
forfeit is *buying* you another necessity: the resolution of the
problem. You may have to be mature enough to say, 'Too bad
it cost so much, but at least I've got what I want now. I've got
peace of mind, and stability.'

CHAPTER 3

The Child's Day in Court

Up to this point, I have tried to reassure you, again and again, that your child can handle most of the disruptions and problems raised by your divorce, as long as you try to continue the parenting process.

But now I must turn to an aspect of the divorce that your child very likely *cannot* handle: testifying in court as a part of a custody fight – a battle to determine who will have custody of the children.

When parents ask me how to deal with this situation, I usually answer, 'Don't.'

'What kind of an answer is that? What on earth do you mean?'

'I mean, don't. Don't do it. Don't go to court in the first place. Settle it out of court.' And if I thought that enough of you would listen, I would be tempted to end this chapter right now, with that single piece of advice: don't fight it out in court.

Please note that I am talking primarily about going to court over custody – a court battle that could involve the direct participation of the child. I am excluding other possible court action around issues that do not involve the child directly – division of property, for example, or support payments. While I strongly favour mediation of *all* conflicts in the divorce, I am much less worried about those which do not bring the child into court to testify 'for' or 'against' his parents.

When parents expect me to give them a list of do's and don'ts to help them and their children deal with the court appearance, and instead I give them a lecture on the harm they are about to do to their children, and on the benefits of mediation, they often become confused and defensive, and they reach for some stock arguments to convince me (and themselves) that it really is not going to be so bad.

Let's look at some of these arguments. My rebuttals will help you understand why I believe that court appearance is one of the most harmful situations your children will ever face.

Argument 1: 'We know it isn't so good for the kids, but the judge is a very kindly person and the children will be seen in his private chambers just for a short, friendly talk to indicate which of us they would like to live with; so it shouldn't be too traumatic.'

My answer: What is actually being asked of your children by this kindly judge in his 'private chambers'? Look at it from the children's point of view. They are taken to a strange place, placed before a stranger, and asked to trust him. That is what it really comes down to, isn't it? True, the words may come out of the friendly judge's mouth in the form of questions, but what the children really hear is, 'Trust me, I'll make the right decision.' But are the children willing to extend this trust? Look what happened last time they did! The parents they thought were going to live happily ever after have separated. An illusion was shattered, and it will take a long time to get over this. Right now, the children probably do not trust adults, and here we are expecting them to trust someone they have never met before. So the children feel a tremendous vulnerability in this situation. Will their trust be betrayed again?

At the same time, the children also receive an opposite message. They are totally powerful. They are being asked to determine which parent will win their favour, which parent they will choose to live with. (It does not matter if they are asked such a question directly, or if the judge decides what the children really want from the answers they give to other, indirect questions: the children know that their answers will decide.)

So the children feel that they are now saddled with a very big responsibility: determining which parent they will live with and, thus, determining their own future. Except for one problem. Their first choice – 'I'd like to live with both of them' – is going to be ignored. So they have to settle for second best. And that might mean telling one parent that they prefer the other one. This is a tremendous amount of pressure to place on children.

All of us, from early life, have ambivalent feelings towards important people in our life. This is normal. We can experience both love and hate towards the same person. But we cope with this as we mature. Without having openly to choose one feeling over the other.

Now, however, the children are obliged to suppress their loving feelings towards one parent and to say, 'I do not choose you as the main parent.' What a perfect method for fostering guilt, and lowering self-esteem!

So, to avoid feeling guilty, the children try to convince themselves that the 'rejected' parent really was a Bad Person all along. They direct all of their hate against that parent, but this does not prevent the guilt . . . in fact it only makes things worse, because the children used to love this parent, and a good deal of their own personality and identity is bound up in this parent. Soon they are trapped, torn between guilt, hatred, and even self-hatred.

That 'friendly chat' in the judge's chambers, then, is in reality the unleashing of a whole host of mutually conflicting pressures on the children. Power ('I will be making the decision') versus powerlessness ('They won't listen to what I *really* want, which is to have them both back again!'); guilt ('I must be a terrible person if I can reject someone who loves me, and whom I love') versus hatred ('If I rejected that parent, then obviously he/she must be the terrible one, not me').

And all this with a kindly judge! Imagine what might happen if either of your *lawyers* ever got a crack at the children.

Argument 2: 'Okay, so it'll be bad. But how can I just give up and cave in to my ex-spouse's demands? Won't my children stop loving me if I don't fight to keep them? Won't they lose respect for me as their parent?'

My answer: You are afraid that your failure to do battle will somehow erode your stature in your children's eyes. Maybe they will think the other parent wants them more than you do. So the fight somehow becomes a proof that you are discharging your parental responsibilities. You are displaying love (demonstrating to the kids that you really want them), and parental concern for their welfare (by pointing out all the ways in which you are a more qualified parent than your ex-spouse). It is a nice argument . . . but it is pure self-deception.

The truth is the exact opposite: taking the fight to the limit is a form of *abdicating* your parental responsibilities.

One reason is that it usually leaves you too exhausted to be an effective parent. Parenting requires a great deal of emotional energy. Any extra anxieties or pressures deplete that energy. Of course, nobody can avoid all such pressures, but why take on any more than you have to? Worse, why rush out to meet new ones? I have seen it so many times: the court proceedings drain the combatants to such an extent that there is little left over for proper parenting.

More important, though, is the way court battles eventually distort reality ... to the severe detriment of the children. Inevitably, the arguments and animosities become more important than the real-life issues. Words like 'pride', 'saving face', 'giving in', become more important than 'settling', 'resolving', 'what's right for the children'. The children's welfare all too often takes a back seat to the adults' welfare – the need to score points, the need to play out the conflicts that led to the divorce itself (which probably had nothing to do with the children) by winning the ultimate prize, and doing the ultimate damage to the enemy.

And then, as the process continues, something interesting also happens. The adults give up their abilities to talk, to decide, to judge themselves and each other in a fair and mature way. Instead, they have to be represented by others: lawyers speak for them; psychiatrists, social workers, Divorce Court Welfare Officers, guardians evaluate them and testify for them; and finally, judges make decisions for them. The parents have regressed to the point of having to be treated like children! They are no longer in control. Instead of working out rational decisions together, they must now submit to an audience of others, strangers, who will do the deciding. This means they must exaggerate what has really been going on: they have to condemn more than they wish to condemn, they have to 'prove' points – they have to paint the picture.

This problem was effectively dramatised in the book and film, *Kramer versus Kramer*. Remember the courtroom scene? The mother had to paint the father as an unfit father – something she *knew* was untrue. The system manœuvred two sensitive and caring people into saying and doing things they really did not want to do.

Inevitably, the situation creates a total distortion of what each parent actually is, and what each one has represented to the children. You draw a picture of your ex-spouse that even *you* cannot recognise. The price of victory can be the total destruction of the relationship between the children and the parent who lost; between the children and the parent who won (when the children turn on this parent); and perhaps even both relationships, leaving the children, in effect, parentless.

Attack breeds counter-attack, so each parent must submit to being dragged over the coals. Can one ever fully recover from such an onslaught? How does one return to parenting, after all this?

Argument 3: 'If it's that bad, we won't drag the children into court. We'll battle out the custody issue in court by ourselves ... but the children won't know.'

My answer: The children will know.

They can sense the struggle, the preoccupations, the anxieties that both parents feel. They will overhear snatches of conversation from you, from your ex-spouse, from friends and relatives. They will know that something is brewing and, in their self-centred way, they will often assume that they are responsible. We touched on this problem in the chapter about breaking the news of the divorce: you will remember that children often blame themselves for having 'sent' one of their parents away. Now they see the custodial parent anxious about something, something that they sense (rightly) involves them. Does that mean this parent is soon to leave, too? And if so, with whom will the children live? Who will care for them?

I hope I have demonstrated how harmful it is for custody to be decided in court. If the children have to testify, even before a friendly judge in private chambers, the effects can be horrendous. And even if the children are not directly involved, the suspicions and tensions, as we can see above, can be quite damaging.

Are there any circumstances in which I believe you *should* go to court? Yes – where it is clear that the children will be seriously harmed by the *present* custodial situation. For example:

- where a parent is dangerous to the children (for instance, a psychotic parent who may physically harm the children);
- where there is danger that a parent may sexually molest one of the children;
- where it can be shown that the children are displaying symptoms of intense conflict and anxiety *arising out of their relationship with the custodial parent*. This must be distinguished, however, from similar symptoms that are caused by the children's reaction to the parental conflict itself;
- where any of the above situations apply not to the custodial parent, but to that parent's new partner.

In these kinds of situations, where the physical or psychological safety of the children is at risk, you have an obligation to move quickly and resolutely. There is no room for negotiation – the other parent is potentially or actually harmful, and you must have final custody of the children.

But be careful not to take my comments as a licence to attack! Let me stress that in evaluating the conduct of a parent, I am concerned solely with parenting ability *and not with other behaviour or standards of conduct.* It is a very difficult point to defend, I admit, but I believe proper parenting does not necessarily mean living up to all standards set by our society. A person may be guilty of gross misbehaviour in public, suffer from alcoholism, severe neuroses, sexual disorders, or even be guilty of a terrible crime ... yet still be effective as a parent. People who by many standards could be seen as misfits of society can nevertheless be sensitive and empathetic to the needs of their children, effective and dedicated to them. Others who are looked upon as model citizens and pillars of our society may be quite insensitive to their children, and entirely lacking in commitment towards them.

Remember, too, that failure to be a good spouse does not make one a bad parent. Infidelity to one's spouse does not make one a bad parent.

If the other parent lives by certain standards which you would not want your children to follow, your best course is to provide an alternative set of standards, and to point out and explain the difference to the children. Tell them that, while you agree they should be exposed to the other parent because of that parent's fine qualities in certain areas (and don't hesitate to list them), you hope the children will not adopt what you believe to be certain undesirable characteristics or values, just as you hope they don't adopt some of *your* faults. This approach lets you retain your values and thus, your integrity; lets you communicate those values to the children in a direct way; yet does not tangle up the question of the other parent's values or standards with the issue of the parental role.

If you do have to go to court ...

I have told you not to go to court over custody if you can possibly avoid it. I have outlined a few really dire circumstances under which court action may be appropriate, and even here I have tried to suggest extreme caution, so that you are absolutely positive court action is warranted.

You have read what I have to say. You agree. But in spite of everything, you still have to go to court. What now?

1. Sit down with your children and tell them exactly why you are doing this.

2. Allow them to talk to you about their misgivings and fears. They will have plenty of them.

3. Let them know that you realise this hurts them, but that you have to do this because, to the best of your knowledge, and that of your professional advisers, this is the only solution.

4. Follow the rules of discussion that we laid down in previous chapters: stressing at all times that what is happening is *not* their fault; that you recognise how they are being hurt; that you hope they will overcome their hurt and somehow, through discussion, understanding, and working on their feelings, learn something from it.

5. Follow the advice of your professional advisers, as to how much the children are to be told, and how they are to be told, about the mechanics of the approaching court case and their role in it. It may be that these 'technical' explanations should not come from you, but from your lawyers.

6. If the children are going to be required to appear in court, do not get into any discussions or arguments with them about what they are planning to say, what you want them to say, what you do not want them to say. In particular, difficult as it may be, do not condemn them or threaten them if they reveal, by their own behaviour and actions, that they may not be planning to take your side.

7. Do not condemn them for any difficult behaviour at this time. Discipline as usual, but refrain from 'editorial comment'. Try to get them to channel disruptive actions into *words* – and this means, as we have seen before, encouraging them to talk, to express their feelings.

8. When it is all over, explain to them as clearly and simply as possible the results of the judgement handed down.

9. Do not give yourself the relief – and them the anxiety – of reviewing every moment of the court battle, blow-by-blow, and what every witness said about their other parent.

10. If the judgement has gone against you, assure them that this will *not* mean a change in your love for them or your commitment to parenting. They must not be left with the feeling that your commitment to them was dependent on 'winning' in court!

11. Allow them to come to their own conclusions about the results, and the judgement that was handed down. If they want to discuss those conclusions with you, by all means listen and encourage them to express their feelings. But do not try to manipulate them into siding with you. Parents will often do this in an attempt to win the children's sympathy, attention, and support. If you are entitled, and the children want to, fine ... but let it come from them spontaneously. Otherwise, they will simply cater to *your* needs when they tell you that, yes, it's going to be terribly hard on you now that the judge has decided X, Y, Z. Don't think they do not know you are trying to use them, either. They will have worked out what they have to say in order to deal with you. After all, why should they not tell you what they think you want to hear, if it keeps you happy and makes their life easier? You may feel better as a result, but the children will know they have been used and they will resent it. In later years, it could come back to haunt you. So relax, and let the judgements and conclusions flow from them naturally, without prompting, when *they* are ready.

12. When the final court decision is handed down, there may be radical changes in your life. This will require careful explanation to the children and may trigger some new emotional problems for them. I will deal with these as a separate topic, in the next chapter.

The above steps cannot entirely prevent the emotional damage that almost always occurs when the children are dragged through a court battle over custody. If the list looks a bit skimpy, compared to the many 'do's' and 'don'ts' I have given you on some other subjects, it is precisely because there is *not* a lot you can do to make things come out better.

What the above strategy does accomplish, though, is to get some of the children's feelings out into the open *before* they have to go into court. They may not feel any better when they get there, but at least they have had the chance to experience some of the tension, fear and pain *in advance*, and to see that you were there with your support and understanding. While this will not make the court appearance any easier, it will give them a little more emotional security: the confidence of knowing you will be there afterwards, with the same kind of support and under-standing, and that you will help them deal with their emotional turmoil.

The bottom line is that there *will* be scars. If you are forced to go to court, the best you can hope for is to keep those scars to a minimum.

That is why I strongly prefer conciliation or mediation, forced if necessary, by qualified neutral conciliators – social workers, psychiatrists, psychologists, etc. – who can bring problems to a resolution quickly. (Your local Citizens Advice Bureau can give you some guidance in locating a conciliator.) But this involves far-reaching social and legal reforms, and we have to deal with the world as it really is: a world in which you may well find yourself, and your children, appearing in court in a custody fight.

CHAPTER 4

Period of Adjustment

Whether through peaceful mediation or a contested court battle, your divorce has now worked its way through the system. Judgement has been rendered, and you have been handed a divorce decree. Issues like custody, visiting rights, maintenance, etc., are now finalised.

This may mean changes in your living arrangements. Certain decisions that may have been agreed upon during the separation stage could now be altered, sometimes radically. You may now have joint custody, where previously you had sole custody. You may now have more access to the children than you did before. Or less. Or none at all. There may be special problems – geographical distance, changes in standard of living, even changes in surname.

How do you explain all this to the children? What special needs do they have right now? What problems should you be alert to? Which ones are natural, disappearing with time, and which ones may require special attention? These are some of the questions I will deal with in this chapter.

But first, let us summarise some of the major types of custodial arrangements usually decreed in divorces. The chances are that your particular settlement will fall into one of these categories.

1. *Custodial parent – no access*. One parent retains custody of the children, and the other parent is not allowed any contact with them.

This effectively cuts off any relationship between the children and the non-custodial parent. Obviously, this is a very extreme measure, but one that is believed to be the most beneficial by some very well-meaning, knowledgeable and respected authorities in the field, usually because they feel that the children cannot maintain a positive contact with both parents. (The other common reason – the other parent poses a blatant physical or emotional threat to the children's welfare – does not concern us here. When the children's safety can only be secured by denying access to the threatening parent, this step, while extreme, can be readily justified.) The feeling is that the children's conflicts of loyalty may have a devastating effect on them and on their relationship with both parents. To avoid that conflict, the non-custodial parent is denied access.

There are two strong, and in my opinion decisive, arguments against this approach:

a If we follow this approach to its logical conclusion, then children should not be given any choices anywhere; *all* conflicts should be avoided. We thus deny the adaptability of the normal healthy child.

b In addition, denial of access to one parent usually has a much more serious effect on the children than would any conflict of loyalties. Children usually feel

● that they are to blame for the loss of the outside parent;
● that that parent has wilfully left or rejected them;
● that the custodial parent is to blame for the child's loss of, or rejection by, the other parent;
● some combination of all three.

It is an extremely heavy load for the children. With the exception that I have already mentioned – the non-custodial parent's clear danger to the children – I see this arrangement as far too harsh. It deprives the children of the positive contributions that the outside parent could, and should, make.

From this extreme, there follows a whole spectrum of other custodial situations.

2. *Custodial parent – limited access.* Here there is a custodial parent, and the other parent's access is essentially at the whim of the custodial parent.

3. *Custodial parent – conditional access.* Here access is determined by how the non-custodial parent meets certain conditions or requirements. e.g. supervised access.

4. *Custodial parent – defined access.* Here the non-custodial parent has absolute right to access, and possibly very frequent and regular access. But the terms are very carefully, and very specifically, defined.

5. *Joint custody*. Both parents maintain custody of the children, and share in the major decisions concerning them. In this situation, custody means 'control', but does not necessarily mean equal physical access. The children may live with one parent, and contact with the other parent will be maintained through regular visits. The parents may work out which of them is to have the final say on certain issues – day-to-day discipline, money, education, etc.

6. *Shared parenting or 'co-parenting'*. This is another form of joint custody. The children spend an equal time with each parent. In some cases, the children remain in the principal residence and the parents take turns moving in and out of the house. In other cases, the children move back and forth between the residences of each parent. These 'shifts', whether by the children or the parents, can take place semi-weekly, weekly, monthly, or even yearly. Depending on the maturity and flexibility of the parents, and on their ability to overcome certain practical problems (time, distance, money, schedules), I prefer this arrangement.

There has been criticism levelled against any and all of these arrangements. Each one can have its problems. But, in my opinion, the more restrictive arrangement should be used only as a last resort. If one parent could pose a physical or emotional threat to the children's well-being, or if the relationship between the parents is such a vitriolic one that contact between them is simply impossible, then this extreme arrangement may be necessary, in order to avoid the harm the children would suffer. But such a decision should not be arrived at lightly. Other possibilities should be explored. Could a neutral person serve as 'middle-man', to pick up and deliver the children? Would conciliation or psychotherapy for one or both parents alleviate the problems, and pave the way for the non-custodial parent to gain access?

At the other end of the spectrum, co-parenting is not without its problems either. People who attempt this process must be prepared to do a great deal of work with each other; to have a basic trust in each other; and to believe strongly in their children's needs for both parents. They must be able to communicate very clearly with each other – and even with the best will in the world, they must be ready for many misunderstandings that will have to be resolved. Co-parenting is a huge undertaking. It is not particularly efficient and it can, therefore, be exhausting. It presupposes a tremendous amount of dedication to the children, as it demands a great deal of effort and sacrifice.

Does it work?

Co-parenting is a fairly new way of dealing with child custody: as to results – the jury is still out. The children definitely receive more than the usual amount of parental attention. In my view, the outcome depends a great deal on the quality of this parental attention. Parents have to guard against over-indulging the children, or allowing them to play one parent off against the other. But if co-parenting is carried out with sensitivity to the children's needs, then they will thrive. Co-parenting can increase the children's self-esteem, because it provides them with constant proof of how important the children are to their parents. I also feel that children profit most through exposure to both adults. A single parent too often has to try to supply everything to the child (leading to exhaustion), and the child may begin to feel that he too will have to grow up to be an all-powerful super-parent.

Although I have stated my own preferences and dislikes, I do not want you to be unduly worried if your particular custodial arrangements are not in one of my favourite categories. This does not mean your children cannot enjoy effective parenting. In fact, in a great many cases, spanning all forms of custodial arrangement, I have seen couples – *once the divorce was finalised* – actually become better parents.

There can be many reasons for this, but the most typical are:

- the guilt feelings they may still have about the divorce, leading to a sharper awareness of the parental role;
- an increase in feelings of responsibility towards the children, partly caused by the shock of realising that the physical separation really *is* permanent now;
- new freedom to concentrate on being a parent, now that the divorce fight itself is over;

• competition with the other parent: the divorce battle now over, the fight becomes 'Let's see who can be a better parent, that so-and-so or me.'

The motives, then, can be either positive or very negative, but in the interests of the children, let's not quibble too much as yet.

The final arrangements, whatever they are, represent permanent (and possibly new) ones for the children, and so your first job is to explain this to them.

1. Do it together.
2. Tell the children that you and the other parent have agreed on how to deal with them, and that you are ready and willing to support each other in your dealings with the children.
3. Tell them that if and when the two of you disagree, you will try, as far as possible, to work this out.
4. The children may have a lot of legitimate questions, which should be answered as specifically as possible. But if, in the questioning and the discussion, you notice that they are trying to play one of you off against the other (and they *will* try this), confront them with their behaviour and tell them, firmly, that you will not allow it. Repeat that you and the other parent have already agreed to work together, and to be supportive of one another.
5. Review the arrangements. Cover them step by step, repeating them as often as is necessary for the children to understand. The nature of your explanation will, of course, depend on the age and maturity of the children.

For children under the age of two, you can only use the very simplest terms. You may not be able to explain things at all. The children will require actions, not words. This means a lot of physical contact – holding, hugging, kissing, soothing reassurances in which your tone of voice and your overall demeanour are even more important that the words themselves. To the extent that you do offer words, the messages they want to hear are:

• that you care for them;

- that you will be there, either all the time (if you are the custodial parent) or at certain times (if you are the outside parent);
- that you will do certain things with them/for them.

On this last point, you may have to be very specific, and itemise the things you will be doing: feeding them, changing their clothes, their nappies, giving them baths, helping them go to the toilet, etc.

If you are the outside parent, you will have to be very specific about visiting dates. Mark the visiting dates on a calendar, and then show them very concretely how many days there are between each visit. One good technique is to give them two boxes, one empty, and one filled with a number of blocks equal to the days between visits. Tell them to remove one block from the full box each day, and put it in the empty box. When the full box becomes empty, that will be the day of your visit – *and keep to your dates!*

Older children can recognise the dates on the calendar, and can be encouraged to check off the days. These children do not require the same reassurances about their basic needs – food, clothing, etc. – but will need reassurances:

- that they will be able to keep their appointments for certain weekend activities that they are now engaged in (sports, clubs, etc.) – and that you will in fact take them there and bring them back;
- that there are kids their own age in the visiting parent's neighbourhood;
- that you will allow friends to accompany them on visits, etc.

In other words, older children, who are already taking on certain independent activities and experiences, will focus on how the divorce will get in the way of this emerging independence. They will be concerned about your ability to keep to the schedules, to co-ordinate your efforts with those of your ex-spouse. Many of these concerns can be minimised if you were already doing a good job during the separation stage, and if the final divorce arrangements do not radically alter what went on during that separation period.

Older children are also likely to want to discuss the possibility of reconciliation. They will want reassurance, one more time, that they were not to blame for the marriage's failure, and that they will not be 'abandoned' by either parent, even though one is now permanently out of the house.

The teenager will most likely be fairly independent of both of you, and will probably require relatively little explanation or reassurance as to the impact of the divorce on the physical and logistical details of everyday life. The teenager is also likely to be fairly vocal in passing judgement on the whole situation, now that the divorce is final. On the one hand, you may be harshly condemned, and informed that in this (as in all other areas) you are showing how little you follow your self-professed ideas. On the other hand, your teenager may express bewilderment as to why the two of you put up with such unhappiness for so long, thus siding with your move.

Do *not* be surprised if alliances are formed within the family. Father and son may line up against mother and daughter, or vice-versa. All of these relationships occur, let's not forget, in an ever-changing kaleidoscope as your sons and daughters struggle with their own identities and with the normal developmental problems of adolescence and young adulthood. It is interesting to see how supportive and understanding of their parents may teenagers become, partly due, I believe, to their own struggle for independence at this stage of their development. They are in some ways less shattered by a divorce, because the demands it places on them fit into their position, in their present quest for an independent identity, especially in relation to parents and home.

Once the explanations have been made, your actions as loving, responsible parents are what count. It may be useful to repeat a few general rules that were introduced in the chapter on separating. They apply even more once the divorce is finalised.

1. There should be as little change as possible in the lives of the children. If possible, stay in the same house, and keep the children in the same school.
2. Maintain the same schedule of activities, and try to

duplicate the same lifestyle. (This second point must be taken into account when the property and other financial aspects of the final divorce settlement are discussed: the divorce should not impose any undue financial hardships that will affect the children's day-to-day life and standard of living.)

3. Maintain the same household routines, chores, standards of discipline, hours for various activities. Keep the daily living pattern as 'normal' as you can.

4. Let the children know the benefit of their sharing, not only with you but also with the other parent, the details of what is going on in their lives – the news, the accomplishments, the disappointments. If you are the custodial parent, encourage them to call the other parent, so that the contact is not limited to visiting days. Children get added satisfaction from being able to share news while it is still 'hot' and exciting, so if your child comes home from school to tell you that he 'came top' in an exam, get him to phone the outside parent and share the triumph. Encourage the other parent to phone the children too.

5. Tell the other parent about any problems you are having with the children. You should be partners in the 'hard work' part of being parents, as well as the recreational part.

6. Make sure both of you participate in all the activities that are important to the children (special events, sports, etc.).

Special Situations

The advice I have given you above, on explaining the final divorce settlement, and starting the 'new life', will fit most situations. But there are some special problems that can occur when the divorce settlement imposes some radical changes in the previous lifestyle – new home, new town, new school, different standard of living. You should still follow what I have already said, but there are a few additional strategies and techniques to be aware of.

Essentially, balance two things: be very factual and specific with the children, so that the 'radical change' is very clearly described and there are no surprises later; and secondly, find out the children's attitudes towards the situation, as a means of encouraging them to express their feelings. It is a difficult and delicate balance, because in encouraging the children to express their viewpoint, you do not want to create the impression that this radical change is amendable or negotiable.

Here are the things you should do:

1. Explain to the children the nature of the change, and the reason why. Deal strictly with facts, and do not try to rationalise or justify what has happened. The divorce is a fact. It cannot be changed. It is final. And here is one of the changes – new home, new standard of living, or whatever – that the divorce has caused. The news might be a shock, and might be very disturbing, but the child will be better able to deal with it if there is at least no ambiguity.

2. Don't blame your ex-. Don't assign blame at all, but if some feelings of blame do emerge – and it can sometimes be hard to keep them away altogether, especially in the face of the child's plaintive 'Why?' – then blame the divorce itself, which is another way of saying that *both* parents are responsible.

3. Tell the children that blaming won't help. What counts is action. The *facts* of the radical change are final. The change *will* take place. But what can be done to cope with it? What can the children do? What can the other parent do? By asking the question, you are opening up the possibility of successful coping; without backing away from the finality of the situation, you are re-focusing the child's attention on *positive action now*.

4. Having raised the question of what can be done, ask for the children's input. Encourage practical suggestions. Make some of your own, to get the ball rolling. Plan it *together*. Try to anticipate with each child some of the problems and difficulties that will be imposed by the change. Review possible solutions. Look for the opportunity to follow some of the child's suggestions.

5. Encourage each child to express his or her inner feelings with you: the doubts, the conflicts. Show how some of the practical suggestions you developed together can alleviate these doubts or conflicts. But remember, there is a positive value in the expression – for its own sake – of these feelings, since it unveils them and prevents their being channelled into other, more harmful forms. The practical suggestions can help, but do not feel compelled to talk the child out of *having* doubts and fears in the first place.

6. Share some of your own feelings with each child. Be careful not to overburden the children, however.

7. Be prepared for temporary regressive behaviour as each child adapts to the radical change.

There are some additional points to be aware of when the 'radical change' takes the form of a geographical move. I am assuming that such a move is unavoidable. If there is the slightest chance that it *is* avoidable, then your first step is to back-track a bit and look at all the options. Is it worth it? Is there any other way?

If you conclude that there is no choice, then follow the above steps when you explain it to the children, but also look for an opportunity to compare this situation with a similar one you may have gone through as a child. This is a particularly effective technique with younger children. Share with them anecdotes of your own childhood, and the feelings you experienced on moving into a new neighbourhood, going to a new school, making new friends, etc. Explain the mixed feelings you had – fearing it, looking forward to it, wondering what to do about it.

Ask them how you, as a child, could have gone about solving some of the problems you have just told them about. This makes them active participants – and since, for the moment, they are concentrating on someone else's problem, it is a little less intimidating than their own problems of today. So they are likely to open up and, as their ideas start flowing, they will get a sense of control over this kind of problem. They will gradually transfer that feeling to their own situation, and see themselves less the victim and more the master.

Remember that the real problem they are experiencing when confronting a geographical move is not so much the practical difficulty or fear of the unknown, as their fear of feeling rejected and abandoned by the other parent. And this feeling, in turn, has its roots in what is essentially a *passive* experience: someone, or some circumstance, has done this *to* them, and they could do nothing about it. This sense of impotence only intensifies the emotion.

The key to overcoming the problem is to replace the notion of impotence with a notion of power: to take an active position, to do things that master the situation and reduce the feeling of being overwhelmed by it. The greater their input, their suggestions – either vicariously, in solving your childhood problem, or realistically, in solving their own current problem – the more they will feel themselves in control of the experience.

But even with this technique, the experience may be overwhelming, especially if the move covers a great distance and projects them into a completely different 'world'. So point out to them that you recognise how hard it is, and that one way to make it easier is not to try handling the whole thing all at once. Encourage them to handle each situation, each feeling – and indeed, each day – as a separate unit. Experience it, deal with it, and then go on to the next instalment.

For younger children you can make the advice more vivid by illustrating it. Take them outside, for example, and prop a ladder up against the house. Then say to them: 'If I told you to jump up on to the roof, you would think I was crazy, right? But do you think you could do it by climbing the ladder one step at a time?' They will get the point.

You should also point out to them that many other children have been, and are, in a similar position, and have gone through the same kinds of feelings. The children are not 'freaks' for having divorced parents, for having to move somewhere else.

Some important 'don'ts' in this situation:

1. Don't lose patience with them and accuse them of discussing their feelings too much;
2. Don't just 'sympathise' – *empathise*;
3. Don't try to cheer them up by avoiding all discussion of their problems;
4. Don't tell them not to talk about their problems because you are having enough difficulty with this on your own;

5. Don't burden them with all the emotional problems you
may be encountering right now;
6. On the other hand, don't totally deny that you are
having any problems. Be honest about your own feelings, even
as you encourage the children to express theirs. Just use good
judgement: how old are the children? how much do they
understand? how much can they handle? when does your
outpouring of feelings become over-whelming for them?
7. Don't blame either the children or your ex-, for the present
predicament.
8. When the move is complete, and you are living in the new
environment, don't try to hurry along the process of adapting.
It will take a lot of time and patience. You can't really 'make' it
happen; you have to 'let' it happen. You can help it along, of
course, by trying to re-create, as much as possible, the
conditions that prevailed in the previous home, particularly
those that are not dependent on *where* you live: household
routines, chores, bedtimes, rules and regulations. They can be
carried with you into practically any environment. Another
way is to go back to some of the suggestions the children came
up with when you were asking for their advice. 'Son, you said
that once we were in our new house, you would try to do X
and that wouldn't make you homesick for the old place. Well,
let's try it.' These techniques can ease the transition process,
but they cannot *force* the adapting process to any great degree.
Be patient!

CHAPTER 5

Co-parenting

In most divorce situations, the parent who has left the home will continue to see the children.

This on-going contact can take many different forms. Sometimes, the parents arrive at arrangements with the courts simply formalising what they themselves have worked out. Sometimes, the arrangements are dictated by the courts in an atmosphere of considerable conflict and hostility.

Since there are so many different possibilities, and we can so quickly become bogged down with complicated definitions, exceptions to the rule, qualifying phrases, etc., I will deliberately simplify things a bit, for the purposes of this chapter.

1. I will use the word 'visits' to describe *all forms* of contact between the children and the parent who has left the home.
2. I will assume that the children are still living at home with one parent.
3. I will assume that the children physically leave the home on a periodic basis – weekly, bi-weekly, monthly – to spend time with the other parent, who will be referred to as the 'visiting parent'.

My definitions, while somewhat arbitrary, still do fit the majority of cases, and should make it much easier for me to describe – and for you to understand – the most important aspect of continuing contact with the children, which is not the logistics or arrangements, but the psychological problems and opportunities that are presented to both parents, and to the children themselves. If you are involved in joint custody, for instance, and the children are spending equal time with each parent, the term 'visit' is a little inadequate. Yet many of the problems you are likely to encounter are covered.

I want to start with an opinion, based on my years of experience:

Visits offer more potential for both good and bad, for both improving and damaging the parent–child relationship, than does any other single aspect of your divorce.

Visits establish the continuity of parenthood, building emotional bridges to replace the physical ones that have been removed. They prove to the children that you were telling the truth when you promised that, just because the marriage was ending, it did not mean the parenting would have to end too.

For the parent who has left the home, visits, in fact, *are* parenting.

But even for the custodial parent, whose role is a passive one ('letting them go'), visits provide an important opportunity. By not interfering with the visits, this parent is showing the children that the adults' conflict (which may still be very intense) can and will be put aside for the sake of ensuring the children's relationship with *both* parents. And the children understand this: 'Mummy must really love us if she's willing to let us spend so much time with Daddy, whom she doesn't love any more.' A co-operative and supportive custodial parent shows the children that their relationship with both parents is natural, strong, deep-seated ... and important to the parents themselves.

Almost unlimited potential for good. But there is another side.... For the visiting parent, there is the chance to belittle and sour the environment in which the children are living during the rest of the week or month. There is the chance to bribe, cajole, wheedle information, strut and seek to impress, downgrade the efforts of the custodial parent, complain, berate, confuse – even destroy.

For the custodial parent, the situation is unfortunately just as fertile. There is the chance to instil in the children guilt, fear, loathing, shame, or other negative emotions. There is the chance to play – choose your favourite role – victim, martyr, overseer, judge, destroyer. There is the chance to warn, thwart, prevent, spy, scold, manipulate.

And for the children, there is the chance to keep secrets, watch every step, pretend, curry favour, 'tell on', blackmail. Almost unlimited potential for harm. That the same situation should have such diametrically opposite possibilities is not

altogether surprising. All of the pressures of the divorce itself –
many of which have nothing to do with the children – are
poured into this one transaction. The wife brings her fears and
anxieties, the husband his, and the children are left to navigate
the minefield, keeping one eye on 'peace at home', and one eye
on 'enjoy this visit with Daddy'. The fact that the visiting
arrangements are usually very formalised, the result of specific
and often severe negotiation, only makes things that much
more intense. In such an artificialised exposure of child to
parent, it is difficult – often impossible – to be natural. Yet, as
we shall see, being natural is the only way to take advantage of
the potential for good, and eliminate the potential for harm,
that visits represent.

The dynamics of visits can best be understood by starting
with a look at how the parents and the children often feel just
before a visit.

With what hopes do they approach each visit? With what
anxieties? What's in it for them? What do they hope to gain?
What opportunities are they aware of, and what problems do
they fear? What opportunities, and problems, may they be
unaware of?

The Custodial Parent

For the custodial parent, the visit is seen as a passive experience. The other parent is in charge . . . for better or worse. The
custodial parent's role is, all too often, limited to worrying *before*
the visit, and undoing the effects of the other parent *after* the
visit.

Let's listen to three different mothers talk about visits. The
first has permanent custody of the children; the divorce has
been completed. The other two have temporary or interim
custody, pending the final divorce settlement in the courts. In
all three cases, the father comes once a week, 'collects' the
children and takes them out for the day, and returns them at the
prescribed time.

- 'Every Friday night, I can't fall asleep, thinking that
  tomorrow is *it*, the day, visiting day, when Mickey comes.
  Sometimes I think he's going to come in a jet plane and

sweep them all away – I know it's like a fantasy, me imagining that he does something really extreme, takes them off to France for the day, or something like that. But that's Mickey's style, he's so extravagant, he just splashes money all over them – I mean, how can I compete with that?'

- 'All he does is tell my two daughters what a tramp their mother is. Last week, my thirteen-year-old comes home from his place and asks me if I'm using birth control when I go to bed with my boyfriend! Guess where she got that idea from.'

- 'It's funny, because Warren and I didn't have a messy split-up or anything like that, and we talked everything over very carefully, the access and all that stuff. I never anticipated any problems, but Warren somehow just keeps trying to make little Robbie over in his own image. I send the kid out in jeans and a T-shirt, and Warren brings him back at the end of the day in a different outfit. One day, Rob told me his Daddy gave him a lecture about dirty fingernails! Who cares about something like that? The child's only five, after all, and *I* certainly don't pay any attention to his fingernails. But that's Warren for you . . .'

I have chosen these three quotations very carefully, because although the specifics are different, all three exemplify the most common problem of the custodial parent: *they see the other parent as a threat to their position, and to the everyday security they have been trying to create.*

Viewed in this way, the visit loses all connection with the welfare of the children themselves. It becomes another skirmish in the battle for supremacy, with the children as incidental pawns.

Sometimes this attitude is acknowledged openly, with not even the pretence of concern for the children's welfare. Look at the second comment. The woman could not have been more blunt in seeing the visit *only* in terms of her battle with her husband. His attack on her reputation is the only meaningful aspect of the visit; the visit's effect on the children is of no concern to her.

More often, though, this view of the visit as an extension of the separation/divorce struggle is very insidious and difficult to root out, because it *does* get expressed in terms that have to do with the (real or imagined) welfare of the children, and therefore *can* be rationalised as being the thoughts of a 'good mother', rather than the jealousies and anxieties of a contestant for power.

The first mother, for instance, complaining about her husband's extravagance, imagines herself to be a 'good mother', worried about her children being spoiled by the father's over-indulgence. Her concerns, if we take them at face value, are certainly valid, and it would be difficult for an impartial observer to defend the free-spending tendencies of the father. Thus the mother fools herself into believing that her tensions are based exclusively on a concern for the children. A closer look at her language and tone, however, shows clearly that the real issue is her fear of not being able to 'compete' with her husband.

The third mother experiences the same problem, packaged somewhat more subtly. Here the husband's actions may seem extreme – he changes the clothes the child is wearing – and the wife's response, while disapproving, seems mild, certainly not neurotic, and expressed almost with a bemused sense of humour. But look at the language more closely:

'I send the kid out in jeans ... Warren brings him back ...

'I never anticipated any problems ...

'Robbie told me his Daddy gave him a lecture ... who cares? *I* certainly don't pay attention to his finger-nails ...'

Where is the *child* in all of this? How does *he* feel about having his clothes changed? About the lecture from his father? Is it good for him or bad for him? Is the mother even aware that he may have feelings on the subject? We do not know. It is not part of her description of the situation.

For her, the visit is simply a matter of: I did this, Warren did that. Her closing line, 'But that's Warren for you ...' foreshadows what eventually became of this situation in real life: a few seemingly trivial differences that emerged during the early visits quickly escalated into a desperate, no-holds-barred battle for control of the child.

In all three examples, then, the mother viewed the father's

visit as primarily the arrival of an external threat to herself. This is not to say that the father was doing no harm to the child or children, and that the mother should not have been concerned. And I am certainly not saying that, in real life, all custodial parents are oblivious to the children's welfare and preoccupied with their own. The fact is, however, that in all too many cases the children's interests take second place. The 'challenge' that the outside parent represents is seen not as a damaging influence on the *children*, requiring *parental* reaction from the custodial parent, but rather, as an extension of the original marital conflict, requiring a 'divorced person' reaction.

The Outside Parent

The visiting parent confronts the mirror image of the same issues: the visit offers a brief, intensive period of time in which to gain popularity, assert influence, or even establish control.

Because the visit is usually brief, it is easy for everything to become exaggerated. The pace of activity can all too often become almost frenetic, leaving the children exhausted (but the benefactor very self-satisfied); simple problems can become major ones that must be Totally Solved Right Now ... because, after all, it will be a full week/two weeks/month before contact is made again.

Some of the problems are dramatically illustrated in these typical comments from parents without custody:

- 'The hard part is, I don't see them every day, and when I finally do see them and they don't have a good time, I really get worried. A few weeks ago, I took them to the cinema and it was a total disaster – they hated the film, the youngest one spilled coke on herself and started to cry ... anyway, after the film I couldn't get them to do anything. They didn't want to go to the zoo, which was the other thing I had planned. I finally took them home early, and Marilyn didn't say anything, just kind of glared at me, and I felt really disappointed with myself.'
- 'He never helps my son with his homework. He's a bright kid, but sometimes he needs a little help. I always ask him

about it, and it really bothers me that John won't work with him. So finally, last weekend, I worked out a whole schedule with him for how much work he gets every night, and I told him to insist that his dad sit down and help him. And then, just to make sure, I talked to John about it when I took him home. He got all mad and accused me of trying to turn the kid against him. Frankly, I don't care if he gets mad, as long as he spends the time with my son on his homework.'

- 'I had the kids for the whole weekend, and I don't think I ever had so much fun. Them, too. I let them stay up to watch television – the seven-year-old fell asleep in my arms – and we bought this enormous pizza! But you can't win, right? I take them back home on Sunday afternoon, and Barb goes through the roof! What did I think I was doing, she screams, letting them stay up so late? I got so mad, I almost punched her in the mouth. Look, if they don't know that a visit to Dad means having a good time, what am I accomplishing?'

As with the other comments, I have chosen these three statements very carefully, to reflect the problems and tendencies that are most frequently observed in outside parents.

First, the visiting parents *appear* to be very concerned about their children. I have rarely met one who is overtly indifferent, neglectful, or unfeeling. In some cases, this apparent parental concern for the children turns out to be rooted in fear, in the parent's belief that anything less than 'best behaviour' with the children might mean losing access to them. This fear makes that parental concern a little less genuine, perhaps. But in most cases, the concern is absolutely sincere. On the surface, then, it looks like no problem – three good parents who just want to be with their kids, and show the kids a good time.

But when we look under the surface, we see the same disturbing tendencies that we saw when we listened to the earlier trio: these parents see the situation, and use the situation for *themselves*, as part of their marital and divorce conflict.

Let's take the last parent first. What's really going on, underneath all his good-time joviality? Is this father really interested in having fun with the children for *their* sake? Or does letting them stay up late serve to establish him as their 'favourite', in contrast to the more discipline-conscious mother?

The clue to his real motives comes in his reaction to the wife's harsh criticism. He does not defend his actions as being good parenting. He does not justify late hours and large quantities of pizza as being benefits to the *children*. Instead, he counter-attacks ('I almost punched her in the mouth') and justifies his action in language that is undeniably self-serving: 'If they don't know that a visit to Dad means having a good time, what am I accomplishing?' His 'accomplishments' are seen only in terms of his ability to score points with the children, at the expense of his wife. If no points are scored, the visit 'accomplished' nothing.

And what about the second parent, who is so concerned about her son's homework? Is it really the homework that is at issue? Look at her actions. She does not discuss the problem quietly and privately with her husband – something she would do if her sole concern were the welfare of her son. Instead, she airs the problem openly in front of the son – almost eagerly, in fact. She virtually orders the son to pass along her instructions to the husband, to insist that he help the son with his homework. She is more than happy to take the argument right to his doorstep, now that she has made sure the son is clued in to the conflict. It is clear that the homework is not an issue of purely *parental* concern, but is really just a lever to set off another attack on the husband. We are entitled to be suspicious of her motives, when we consider the eagerness with which she enters battle, and the speed with which her comments shift from the son ('He's a bright kid ...') to the husband ('It really bothers me that he won't work with him. . . . Frankly, I don't care if he gets mad ...'). Is she acting like a mother? Or like the embattled party to a divorce?

The first father's comments present the most subtle of the three problems – and for that reason, the most difficult one to identify and solve. He takes the children for a day, and things just don't work out. In fact, he calls it a 'total disaster'. The children did not enjoy the film. One of them spilled a soft drink. They were obviously fidgety and irritable. He feels tremendously disappointed, and it is hard for us not to sympathise with him. He comments briefly on his wife's reaction to his early return – 'Marilyn didn't say anything, just kind of glared at me ...' – but he does not criticise her or attack her.

Where is the problem, then? Surely he is a decent, sincere man who has suffered a perfectly understandable disappointment? Surely I have made a mistake, in lumping him in with the other two, as representative of a 'problem'?

Look again. There is no sign that he is thinking about how his *children* reacted to the day. He is certainly entitled to be disappointed for himself – any of us would be – and it is absolutely okay for him to tell us so. But why not also comment on his children's feelings? Were *they* particularly upset? Was it a 'total disaster' for them, too? Do they get 'really worried' when they do not have a good time, as their father apparently does?

And where does it say that every day has to be a 'good time' in the first place? A relaxed, confident parent, carrying out a normal, spontaneous relationship with his children, knows that not every day is fun. Children can become bored and irritable, and parents who are not operating under the pressures of a separation or divorce are usually able to take these 'off days' in their stride, and not read into them any out-of-proportion significance.

But not this father. It is clear that he has set up artificial and exaggerated expectations for the visits – expectations which speak almost entirely to his own emotional turmoil, and in particular, his sense of loss. He is not dealing with the real world of the children themselves. For him, everything must be perfect. Everything must be fun. There must be a whirlwind of activity – if not the cinema, then the zoo; if not the zoo, then something else. The day cannot be permitted just to be frittered away, or to end inconclusively.

It is the *father's* needs that are being served by this desire for a fairy tale with a happy ending.

All of the people I have described are human. Under the stress of divorce, of a drastically different lifestyle, they have made mistakes with their kids. That is understandable. But it could have been avoided.

*   *   *

One of the earliest, and most common, outward signs of the fears and tensions that are bubbling under the surface is argument between the parents about the visiting arrangements themselves.

These arguments are actually a quick and convenient transfer of the real power struggle into a more palatable form. It is easier to say, 'I don't want you to bring Robbie back home so late', than it is to admit, 'I want to assert my power over you, and Robbie's a great way to do it.'

Almost as soon as the separation takes place and the visits begin, it will be quite common to find the parents bickering about the arrangements, about the shirking of responsibilities, about the aftermath of a particular visit. If you are having these kinds of arguments, check the list below. It is my selection of the 'Ten Top Irritants' in relation to visits, and the chances are good that you will find your pet topic in there somewhere.

1 *Transporting times*
    'You picked them up too early/too late.'
    'You brought them home too early/too late.'
    'You're always turning up at a bad time. Why do you always come right when we're sitting down to dinner?'

2 *Transporting place*
    This argument usually occurs when the parents live far away from each other:
    'I can't come all the way over there and get them; you're supposed to drive them to the corner of A and B.'
    'No way! You want them, you come here.'
    Or this variation:
    'I thought we agreed I was going to drop them off at the corner of A and B – the house is too far away for me.'
    'All right, you don't have to return them to the house. But A and B is ridiculous. At least drive them to the corner of C and D; it's much closer for me.'

3 *Who does the transporting*
    'If you can't come and get them yourself, they're not leaving this house.'
    'There's no way I'm going to let your girlfriend be the one who brings them back home.'

'Your boyfriend better not be there when I bring the kids home tonight. If he is, they're staying with me.'

4 *Meal arrangements*

'You mean you haven't given them breakfast yet? Now I've got to waste an hour taking them to a restaurant!'

'You mean you had them the whole day, and you didn't give them supper before bringing them home? Do you realise how late it is for me to start cooking now? What am I, a slave? Can't I even get one day's rest?'

Or the opposite:

'Why did you give them breakfast? You know I enjoy taking them out!'

'How many times have I told you *not* to give them dinner before you bring them home! You know I always prepare something special for them when they come back.'

5 *Clothing and 'supplies'*

'How could you send them out without a heavy sweater – it's freezing cold at this time of year!'

'What do you mean by sending them out wearing a sweater – it's practically summer, they were boiling hot all day.'

'Why do you always dress them in their good clothes; you know I like to take them to the park to run around.'

'You forgot to give Billy his cricket bat; what was I supposed to do with him all day?'

'I sent them out clean, you brought them back with their clothes all torn and dirty.'

'How could you let him lose his schoolbooks? He had them with him when I gave him to you this morning!'

'A brand new pair of shoes! The child spends one day with you, and boom! They're ruined!'

6 *Changes in the arrangements*

'How dare you phone me at the last minute and tell me you're going to be late? I don't care if you've got an important meeting. You're supposed to be here to pick up the kids!'

'No, I won't come and get them an hour early just because you want to go out with your boyfriend.'

7 *Behaviour of the parents' friends*
  'I don't want them even to *see* that girlfriend of yours.'
  'I don't like what your boyfriend said when I brought them back home.'
  'Every time I come to get them, that nosey friend of yours is there, trying to stir up trouble.'

8 *Activities during the visit*
  'I don't like where you took them this week.'
  'I don't like that film you took them to. I don't want them to see stuff like that.'
  'I've told you I didn't want you taking them over to your mother's. All she does is turn them against me.'
  'This is the fifth time you've taken them skating. I want them to have some variety when they're with you.'
  'All they did today is hang around your apartment watching TV. What kind of a father are you, anyway?'

9 *Unfair 'using' of the children*
  'Why did you tell them to find out how much my apartment is costing me?'
  'They came home and told me you spent the whole day asking them about how many new clothes I've bought. Don't you dare have them spying on me like that!'

10 *Meeting face-to-face*
  Many people can't handle that necessary moment of contact when the children are exchanged. In a really hostile separation, the arguments can start instantly, and about nothing. But even in a relatively amicable separation, this can be a tense moment. Often, one party will be overly solicitous, leaving the other party embarrassed or uncomfortable. Sometimes, one party will be too formal, leaving the other feeling hurt or rejected. This can trigger an argument, over the most convenient issue at hand – today's visit.

It is important to recognise that not every argument is necessarily invalid. The other parent may indeed be doing things that are harmful to the children, or contrary to your ideas. The situation may very definitely call for some response on your part. So I am not advocating total passivity. All I am saying is: examine *your real feelings first*. Why is this argument taking place? Is it because of something that really matters to the children? Something that legitimately involves their welfare? Or is it for yourself? Is it a way of 'getting' at your ex-spouse? Perhaps for the sheer pleasure of it? Or as revenge? Or to relieve your own emotional stress at the failure of your marriage? Perhaps to 'soften up' your ex-spouse so that some aspect of the divorce settlement (money being the most common example) can go your way a little more?

You may think I am being unfair. But in fact, I am just going by the percentages: in the vast majority of cases, *arguments about visits are really arguments about the marriage*. They are not arguments between parents, but arguments between ex-spouses. If yours is not, great. But look at it . . . and be honest with yourself.

The Children

Before going into some specific recommendations about what you should, and should not do with visits, let's take a look at the children themselves.

There is no one dominant attitude that children will display. Many factors can influence the children: their age and emotional make-up, the specifics of the adults' conflict, whether the separation is peaceful or non-peaceful, the duration and frequency of visits, and the parents' abilities to be co-operative and mutually supportive about those visits.

Where there are problems with the children, they usually fall within these main categories:

1. Fear
Fear is the simplest, most elemental response to an unpleasant situation or experience. The children may whine and cry and refuse to leave the home to spend time with the outside parent. Or they may be moody and secretive when returning home after the visit.

Sometimes the fear can be traced back to the divorce itself: the children somehow feel responsible for the failure of the marriage, and this guilt is brought to the surface, or intensified, every time the visiting parent appears.

More often, the fear is associated with the visit itself. The children may not feel directly responsible for the actual break-up of the marriage, but they *do* feel responsible for the tensions that arise between the parents at the moment the children are passed from one parent to the other.

Fear can also be generated when the children tune in to some problems associated with the new arrangements, the new life-styles of the respective parents.

For instance, Tommy, a five-year-old, was brought to me when no one could explain his sudden refusal to see his father. The visits had started out well, and this new behaviour was totally unexpected. The child was almost violently obstinate – he kicked, screamed, cried, literally clutched on to the door of the house.

I was gradually able to discover that the father, after having lived alone for the first several months following the separation, had now acquired a girlfriend. Tommy had seen this girlfriend once or twice, and had 'tuned in' to his father's apprehensions about Tommy's having this knowledge (the presence of the girlfriend violated the terms of the visitation arrangements). Tommy was too young to grasp any of the specifics – he only *sensed* that something was terribly wrong.

In reality, far from not wanting to see his father any more, Tommy actually wanted to see him more often. He loved his father very much. But he was afraid that his own vague know-ledge of this other woman was 'bad', that it would somehow hurt his father, hurt himself. He had picked up a very adult-like pressure, and could not handle it. So his solution was to avoid the problem at all costs.

Tommy's experience is surprisingly typical, and it demon-strates quite dramatically a child's enormous capacity to *sense* the adult-versus-adult game that is often played around visits. Since the child's intuition usually outpaces his experience and his emotional maturity, the result is pressure – and fear.

2. Manipulation

Playing one parent off against the other is a common occurrence with many children, and is part of their normal growth and development even when the parents are not divorced. It serves the child's need to challenge the outside world and attempt to exert some control over it.

This normal behaviour can become particularly acute, however, where there has been a divorce and where the child's access to one of the parents is relatively infrequent.

The infrequency of contact (and even once a week *is* infrequent) gives it a highly artificial, dramatised character. The fact that the parents themselves are not in contact with each other means that the child may know far more about each parent than they do about one another. Add all the other emotionally loaded elements – the parents' own apprehensions and insecurities (which may be easily detected by the child), the child's real or imagined resentment towards the parents for having separated – and you now have all the necessary ingredients for enacting 'I'll tell Mummy ...' or 'Wait till Daddy finds out ...' on a grand, and even vicious, scale.

In some cases, the manipulative behaviour is limited to insisting that one parent make good on the promises of the other. This happens in all households, and its presence in the divorce situation is not necessarily significant. 'Mummy said I didn't have to be home until ...'; 'Mummy said it was all right for me to ...' are examples of this simple form of using one parent against the other. Since the parents' access to one another is more limited in a divorce situation, it can take a little longer to find out if the 'promise' from your ex- is real, or concocted by your child. Otherwise, the problem is not particularly serious.

Often, though, the manipulation turns into downright blackmail, and then it is very serious indeed. This can be particularly true where the child is old enough to 'flesh in' the overall hints he is getting about the adult-versus-adult situation, and supply some concrete information in the place of vague impressions. The vague sense of unease that Tommy felt, aged five, about his father's girlfriend, can become, in a child as young as ten, a realistic understanding of exactly what is going on – and a firm decision to take advantage of the situation by threatening to expose it to the other parent.

3. Discipline problems

Children may have discipline problems, produce poor school-work, etc., all through the divorce process. These problems can become particularly acute immediately before, or immediately after, a parental visit. (*Note:* I am not talking about the normal, and entirely healthy, excitement a child may feel in looking forward to a visit. This excitement may – particularly in younger children – cause some temporary distraction from things like schoolwork, household routines, etc. Behaviour gets a little rambunctious; the child is 'keyed up'. This is perfectly normal, and nothing to worry about.)

When the problems are severe, it is usually because the parental visit is being used to further the aims of the parents . . . *and the child knows*. To understand why this should lead to discipline problems, let's look at the situation from the child's standpoint.

The divorce came as a shock, but the child can adjust to that shock. The reassurance that the parent–child relationship would remain intact was the major comfort for the child. The child believed those reassurances, and now (further proof) here comes Daddy, sure enough, right on schedule, for the weekly visit. So far, so good.

But then some of the things start happening that we talked about earlier in this chapter. The parents start arguing, ob-structing, manipulating. The visits become a source of tension. Worse, they now prove to the child that, contrary to what Mum and Dad claimed, parenting *isn't* going to continue as before; instead, they are just going to use these visits as a club with which to beat each other.

When the child realises this, the search immediately begins for some other way to restore the lost parent–child relationship. How can it be accomplished? How can the child make sure his needs are met?

There is a way. He can *force* his parents to act as parents, by presenting them with a problem that requires parent-like action: in short, he can become undisciplined. He can misbehave. He can under-perform (schoolwork, household chores, whatever). He can be 'bad'. *That'll* get 'em acting like Mummy and Daddy again!

To further guarantee their response, he can time this misbehaviour around the most intensive moment of parent–child contact, a time when father, mother and child are all involved: the visit. That is why discipline problems so often occur just before, or just after, the parental visit. The child is trying to force the parents to act like parents, and to improve his chances of success he's choosing optimum timing. His actions lie much closer to the conscious level than the unconscious level.

Of course, if the situation continues to be a high-pressure one, the misbehaving will soon no longer be limited to just before or after a visit. It may spread out to include large chunks of time spent in each home. Or, if the child is too frightened to act up very much in the home, he will transfer the discipline problems to school, church, or other centres of activity.

Summary

Our look at the attitudes towards visits, through the eyes of the individuals involved, should convince you that the most serious problems occur when the parenting role has been diminished or suspended so that the 'embattled spouse' role can be played out to the fullest.

Obviously, then, the solution to most problems lies in your ability to sustain the parenting role; to make this role the paramount feature of the visit. I have specific suggestions that will help you stick to parenting, and not get side-tracked into unnecessary extensions of the marital conflict. But these suggestions won't work unless you recognise that *visits are about parenting, and not about divorce*.

A good way to put yourself in the proper frame of mind is to re-examine your own concept of the nature of parenthood.

What kind of parent were you *before* your life became so complicated with the turmoil of separation and divorce? Your attitudes toward parenthood may differ from mine, or from your neighbour's, but for most people the *methods* of going about the business of being a parent are surprisingly similar: they are characterised by a naturalness and un-self-consciousness that gradually makes the child comfortable with a constant 'feel' for what his parents are like.

It is this 'feel' that you must seek to re-establish, if it has been interrupted by the divorce process.

More than anything, this feel – yes, it has an almost textural quality – is what tells your child that his relationship with you has not been jeopardised by the radical change in your relationship with your spouse.

Were you, for example, strict about certain things? Then go on being strict about them – do not feel you have to over-compensate for the pain of the divorce, by being more lenient with your children than would have been natural before the divorce.

This is just one example: what we are really talking about is the creation of an overall climate, a mood, that matches as closely as possible what the child was accustomed to before the divorce. The maintenance of this mood, or the re-creation of it if it has been interrupted or lost, is the starting point. Think of it as the setting, the environment, the context, for the specific actions you will take and techniques you will employ.

And now, let's look at some of those actions and techniques.

Custodial parent

1. *Make the transition phase between you and the other parent as pleasant as possible.*
Your children may wish to invite the visiting parent into the house: to see some change in their room (new desk, new painting), show off some school project, etc. Allow this. Help your children play the gracious hosts for a few minutes, if they want to. Offer your ex-spouse a cup of coffee. *Use this time to communicate.*

2. *Tell the visiting parent about what has been going on in your children's lives since the last visit.*
Cover both the joys and sorrows. 'Sarah did really well in a maths test, but the teacher says she needs more help with her

spelling.' 'Billy hurt his knee playing football.' 'Nancy's a little apprehensive about this weekend because she knows you're taking her to visit Aunt Martha.' 'Mike's been having trouble sleeping; he misses you.' If the children are a bit older, they may want to be the ones to tell the other parent. Allow them to do so.

3. *Don't pump the children for information when they come back home.*
Asking for information puts needless pressure on the children. By all means ask them what they did, and if they had a good time. But slant the questioning towards *them* – their experiences, their feelings. Let *them* do the talking, let *them* set the pace for how much they choose to reveal. When you look for information about the other parent, however, you are making things unnecessarily difficult for the children. How are they to respond to questions like: 'What sort of person is Daddy's girlfriend?' 'Does Daddy seem happy?' Do you want the bare facts, with no nuances of interpretation or 'editorial comment'? Do you expect them to understand why you want the information, what it is you are really driving at? Can they meet your needs for both information and interpretation? Almost certainly not.

4. *Get comfortable with the idea of the visiting parent's 'taking over' the children – yes, even if you know he's going to use the situation against you.*
Although there may be some relief at the temporary respite from parenting chores, it is usually still hard to give up the kids, even for a day. If the visiting parent is co-operative and it has been a co-operative separation, there will still be anxieties about mistakes that might be made with the children. Will your ex- remember to take the little two-year-old to the bathroom before and after lunch? Will the eight-year-old return home covered in mud? Will they both be given too many sweets?

Worse, if the situation is hostile, there is the very real possibility that your ex- may use the visit *against you* – and we have already looked at some of the ways this can happen.

It is only natural for you to feel anxious. But put your anxieties aside, and be supportive of the visit. Yes, the outside parent is going to be negligent in some areas that you would not have been. This I can guarantee. Yes, your ex- will do things that you do not approve of. But on purpose? Deliberately to harm the children? I have yet to see it.

All right then – what about doing things deliberately to harm *you*? Yes, this can happen. But they will only continue if the tactic succeeds. And the tactic will only succeed if you act as the injured party.

I will be blunt: if you really care about the children, you may have to put up with some unfair activities from your ex-spouse ... and not retaliate. If your retaliation would damage the visits, then it would hurt your children; if you care about them, you do not want them hurt.

Most parents tell me (particularly when they are in the middle of a struggle for custody) that 'there's nothing I wouldn't do for these kids; I'd make any sacrifice.' Here is your chance.

If you are in the more fortunate position of dealing with a co-operative ex-spouse, in a supportive and relatively peaceful atmosphere, you are still going to have apprehensions. Relax. There are lots of other situations in which your children are exposed to influences different from your own. Somehow, they survive. Do you take issue with your children's teachers? Friends? Coaches? Scout Master or Girl Guide leader? All of them may do or say things of which you do not approve – yet rarely will you intervene. Will you always be able to control your children's reading? Exposure to TV? Food and drug intake? Of course not – and you probably accept these limitations to your control as part of the natural limitations (and risk) of parenthood. Naturally, your influence as a parent will be more important than these outside forces. But there is still room for a lot of variety in their lives, and exposure to this variety – within the context of the values you have already established as a parent.

Let your ex-mate handle it. Whether a co-operative or unco-operative situation, the acid test for your intervention is not whether *you* are being harmed, but whether *the children* are being harmed by what your ex-spouse is doing.

5. *Be cautious and low-key if you do have to intervene.*
If you are convinced that some action or inaction on the part of
your ex-spouse *does* constitute a harmful influence on the children, then you shoud intervene.
   First find out the facts. Do *not* go by rumours; do *not* exaggerate
your own fears and apprehensions around a given issue.
   Determine that what is happening is, in fact, harmful. Get advice
from a neutral expert, such as your doctor, psychiatrist,
psychologist, social worker, clergyman, to find out if the particular activities or circumstances you are concerned about
really are harmful to your children.
   Approach the other parent calmly. At all costs, try to avoid a major
explosion. Contact your ex-spouse, suggest a person-to-person
meeting over a cup of coffee. If that is not possible, talk by
phone. Explain your point of view, try to avoid a power struggle, and try to get both of you focusing on what is best for the
children. *Do not condemn.* Question, and state your opinion.
   Never raise the issue with the other parent when the children are there.

6. *How to avoid the 'Please don't tell Daddy I told you' trap.*
Often, your source of information about potentially harmful
circumstances or activities will be the child himself.
   But a special problem occurs – and with considerable frequency, in my experience – when the child gives you the
information and then begs you for secrecy. He has told you
about something that happened during the visit, and which
could be harmful if it continued (some violation of the custody
agreement's terms, perhaps, or maybe a serious lapse in the
parent's supervision) – but he insists that you do not tell the
other parent about it. He does not want the other parent to
know that he 'told tales'.
   You are now trapped between two equally unattractive
courses of action:
   You can ignore your child's request for secrecy, approach the
other parent, and confront him with your child's information.
If this happens, the two of you will probably fight, and the other
parent will probably condemn the child on his next visit, for
having spilled the beans. This will destroy the child's trust in
you, and damage communication among all of you.

You can heed your child's request for secrecy. This will frustrate you, and increase your anxieties every time there is a visit (because, of course, the problem that the child told you about will not have been resolved). It will also frustrate your child who, despite his pleas for secrecy, was actually hoping that somehow you would work out how to honour the secrecy pledge and yet eliminate the problem!

Don't do either of the above.

Instead, follow these steps:

Listen to your child's descriptions of the circumstances that have him worried. Ask him what he did about it, or did not do about it, by himself. If he has not been able to do anything about the problem by himself, ask him why not.

Empathise with the child, and tell him you understand how difficult this is for him. Offer your help in working out, with the child, how to talk to the other parent about the issue – that is, the child is to do the talking, not you.

If the child still cannot – or does not want to – approach the other parent by himself, offer to accompany him. If the child is still reluctant to be there at all, offer to approach the other parent yourself.

If your child continues to insist that you must not approach the other parent, then bring things to a head. Start by saying that the situation he has brought to your attention is, to the best of your knowledge and judgement, harmful to him. Tell him you realise he must think so too, or he would not have told you about it in the first place. Tell him you cannot and will not allow him to be harmed in this way. Explain that you offered him the above choices because you wanted to help him out; you knew he was worried about the other parent's discovering that he 'told'. But now you will have to handle this with the other parent, because you cannot stand by and see the child harmed. So it boils down to the fact that the other parent must be approached by someone – either the child or you. The child is to make the choice.

Outside Parent

1. *Give the children time to adapt to their being with you.*
They have just said goodbye to the custodial parent. Now they
are in your hands. Do *not* crawl all over them straight away. If
they want to sit for a while in silence, before starting up a
conversation, let them. The children should set the pace.

2. *Remember that their time with you is time away from their regular
routine.*
Your children are entitled to as normal a life as possible. This
means school, extra-curricular activities, friends, etc. These are
components of their 'home base'. When they visit you – as
exciting as that visit may be in some respects – it still means
they are leaving this home base and going to a 'satellite base'.
They may be grumpy about this, discontented, anxious, and
sometimes even reluctant to go with you in the first place.

3. *Don't hassle them because they are discontented.*
Don't accuse them of not liking you, of being ungrateful, of
preferring the other parent, of being spoiled. Recognise why
they may feel anxious. It can be helpful to tell them you
understand how they feel. It may sometimes be necessary for
you to pass up a visit altogether, if that visit gets in the way of
some important event that is taking place in and around the
'home base'.

4. *Don't overwhelm them straight away with your 'plans' for the visit.*
Find out what *they* want to do. Decide what is realistic. Then
compare it with any plans you may have already made. Discuss
it with them, and arrive at the best solution. Remember, it is
not up to you to provide round-the-clock special events and
entertainment. The children have to learn to fend for themselves. Did you constantly entertain them when you were living
at home?

5. *Don't worry if the children don't always have a good time.*
As a parent, it is only natural for you to want your children to
enjoy themselves – and for them to know that you want this.

But it does not follow that enjoyment is always possible. Plans fall through. Things do not always work out as hoped. The children must experience this, as part of their relationship with you – just as they would comfortably have done, had the separation and divorce not occurred. Your worth as a parent does not depend on your ability to keep them smiling every single minute – and they know it. Of course they will be disappointed if things do not work out on one particular visit. Feel free to share their disappointment. But if they see you accept the situation as just another dimension of a natural, unforced relationship, they will feel more secure ... and your relationship with them will have been solidified even further.

6. *Know the everyday pattern of their life, and try to be compatible with it.*
The best way to establish some stability in the children's life, given the disorder a divorce can cause, is to duplicate the same overall life pattern in the households of both parents. When is it bedtime? When does the TV go on and off? How much are the children permitted to use the telephone? What about friends coming to visit? Treats? Pocket money? Homework? Household chores? It will not be possible for you to duplicate literally everything. And the fact that visits are often on weekends means that certain routines that are prevalent during the week may not apply. But duplicate their home routine as closely as you can, and keep checking with the other parent to see that you are up-to-date with the current rules.

7. *Recognise the special needs of each individual child. Vary the visiting pattern if you have to.*
In a normal parent–child relationship, you will often spend time alone with one child, in response to that child's individual needs of the moment. There is no reason why this cannot be done with visits too. Once in a while, you may want to take out just one of the children for some special one-to-one time. Providing you do this judiciously, and do not favour one child at the expense of another, there is no reason why this should cause any problems.

8. *Don't tell them you are lost without them.*
Never say that it is unfair for your ex-spouse to have the children most of the time, that you feel lost or depressed because you cannot be with them every day. You *both* have them – and that is what the children should feel.

However, you certainly can tell them that you miss them when they are not with you, and that you realise they miss you, that that is the unfortunate way things worked out, and what counts is making the best of the time you do have together.

9. *Don't tell them how great you are doing now that you are out of the house.*
This is the flip side of the above point.

Depending on the age of the children, their maturity, their understanding of the circumstances that led up to the separation, you can certainly tell them that you and their other parent were making each other unhappy, that you are happy now, and that you hope (or know) that the other parent is happy, too.

You can also share with them some of the events, ups and downs, of your life as it is now. Travel, your worst football/tennis match yet, funny incidents at work, the routine satisfactions that come along every day – the children can and should know what you are doing, and there is no point feigning depression if you are really doing fine.

But – don't throw it in their faces in a way that makes them wonder if *their absence* is the secret of your success!

10. *Don't try to 'buy' them with gifts, special activities, entertainment.*
This is a common pitfall and it may work for a while, but it sets you up as being worth only whatever material things you can provide. The children will eventually see through these things, and lose respect for you. The test is: is this gift, treat, special entertainment, etc., something you would have done when you were still living at home?

11. *Try to arrange your new living quarters with the children in mind.*
If possible, have a room or rooms for the children to call their own. Include a bed, a desk for schoolwork, toys of their own, etc. If you are in a flat, avoid an 'adults only' building where the

superintendent and the other tenants may hassle you about the children (especially if they are staying the night). Look carefully at the neighbourhood too – is there a park or playground nearby? Potential playmates? Is the area similar to where the children are living now? As much as possible, you want your new home to be their 'second home' – and not just 'a place to visit'.

12. *Try to arrange your schedule so that you can concentrate on your children when they are with you.*
Reality dictates that you may have other things to do during their visit – shopping, working around the house or flat. Let them pitch in and help if they can. If you do have to be occupied somewhere else during their visit, see to it that it is for a very brief time. If that is impossible, discuss the situation with your ex- and see if it is possible to change the time of that particular visit. If you cannot change the time, and you do have to be away for a while, arrange for a sitter – in as responsible a way as you would have done previously – and let the other parent know about it in advance.

13. *Report back to the other parent about any of your concerns for the children that have resulted from the visit.*
This applies especially to any behaviour problems that may have required intervention and disciplining on your part. Let the other parent know. Apart from maintaining a co-operative and supportive role with your ex-, your sharing of this kind of information show *the children* that you are still concerned with, and involved in, their overall development.

Both Parents

1. *Make sure the arrangements for the visit are specific and predictable.*
Time of arrival and time of return should be spelled out clearly, so that everyone knows what to expect. If special arrangements or provisions are required (and it can be as simple as mother's packing kids' raincoats so that father can take them camping), they should be worked out in detail by both of you ... ahead of time. A great deal of unnecessary tension is caused by leaving

arrangements up in the air. It goes without saying, too, that the arrangements should be *achievable*. If you cannot get there by nine in the morning, say so – and make other plans; plans that are clearly understood by all parties *before* the time of the visit.

2. *Don't get into a contest with each other.*
I have talked previously about popularity contests – parental visits seem to promote them with sinister intensity.

Popularity contests cause three main problems:

If it works and you win, you are harming the child. To see why, look at your 'victory' from the child's viewpoint. He now begins to dislike the other parent. Is that healthy? Especially when it may be based on nothing more than your ability to manipulate the child's desire for an ice-cream cone! Look at it another way – if it were not for this divorce, would you be behaving this way, as a thoughtful parent? Of course not.

Chances are it will not work anyway – in which case, you lose heavily. My experience is that most children have no difficulty seeing through these clumsy attempts to curry favour; they gradually lose respect for the parent who is attempting to bribe them.

Worse yet, the other parent may retaliate. And there you will be, the two of you, engaged in a steadily escalating war aimed at proving your popularity with the children. How will you fight this war? By constantly upping the ante. Now instead of one of you being the loser, both of you lose. The children will see through it, and come away with no respect for either of you. They will also begin to manipulate for more things, and develop an attitude that says, 'I am only as good as what I can get from others. On my own I'm not worth much.'

3. *Never discuss the progress of the divorce action.*
Visits seem to trigger bursts of information from both parents about how the divorce is going – what the lawyers have said, impending court appearances, etc. Usually the visiting parent starts, and the custodial parent feels the need to 'set the record straight' when the children come home and repeat what the visiting parent told them. Or the custodial parent may feel the need for a little defensive action in advance of the visit:

'Don't forget, kids, be sure to tell Daddy that my solicitor said ...'

Don't do it. The children should be told as little as possible, and in response to their questions, rather than through parental initiative. Depending on the age of the children, their maturity, and the circumstances of the divorce, the amount of detail you go into will vary considerably. Your own judgement is very important here. Remember, though, that two points must always be clear, whenever the subject comes up:

The children have done nothing to cause the divorce, and can do nothing to prevent or change what will happen.

You will continue to be their parents and act like their parents.

4. *Don't ignore each other's discipline techniques.*
Sometimes, a child is being punished for a 'crime' committed at the home of your ex-spouse, and you are asked to continue the punishment while the child is with you. 'I've told Timmy he can't watch any TV this week.' You have to review your understanding of the crime and its punishment. Discuss the matter with your ex-spouse and with the child. If you agree with the punishment, tell them both that you are in agreement, and then help to carry it out. That part is easy. But what if you *don't* agree with the punishment? Discuss it with your ex-spouse. Question why *that* particular punishment was assigned, and not a different one that you would have meted out. Offer to follow your own type of punishment while the child is with you. If this is acceptable, give the child a full explanation of the switch. Another alternative is to confine the punishment to the child's visits with the other parent.

Sometimes, standards may genuinely differ between the parents. One may demand that the beds be made and the dishes done by the children, while the other does not care. Do not attempt to get into a popularity contest with your ex-spouse. Face the differences openly, and discuss them with the children. Encourage them to abide by the rules of your ex-spouse when they are with that parent, and by your rules when they are with you. Above all, explain to them very clearly that neither you nor your ex-spouse will allow the children to play one set of 'rules' off against the other, to use your standards as a means of avoiding things your ex- may demand, or vice-versa.

5. *Never stop communicating with each other!*
Moods, behaviour, school results, new achievements, health, happy incidents, sad incidents – keep the other parent informed about what is happening when the children are with you. Your primary objective should be to help the other parent do a more effective job of parenting, and information about what you have seen and experienced with the children is a vital tool for the other parent.

Special Situations and Problems
Thus far I have dealt with visits that follow a regular pattern – usually weekly, bi-weekly, or monthly. But there are also certain special occasions or situations that can create very different kinds of problems.
    Such situations include:

1 Religious holidays and ceremonies (Bar Mitzvah, First Communion, Confirmation, etc.)

2 Holidays

3 Birthday parties

4 Family social events (Christmas or Easter, annual get-togethers that have become a 'tradition' and involve both sets of grandparents – and, by implication, both sets of parents)

5 Special events at school (plays, sports days, parent–teacher evenings) or special events associated with the child's extra-curricular activities (music or dance recital, football, Scouts, Brownie events etc.)

6 Half-term and exeats from boarding school

7 Illness of the child or of the other parent

In all situations like these, careful and specific negotiation is required. Will both parents attend the social events? At the same time? Earlier? Later? If possible, the children's own preference should be followed.

It is important to recognise that, even in the best of times and the happiest of families, occasions like these are loaded with emotion, excitement, and even anxiety. It is very unusual to find *any* family gathered at Christmas or Easter, or for a wedding, christening, Bar Mitzvah, etc., and not see tensions, anxieties, the rekindling of old sibling rivalries, and many other cross-currents of emotion and conflict.

So even when things are normal, the pot is bubbling! Now throw in a divorce – and we have the potential for an explosion. How do we prevent it?

Recognise the impossibility of satisfying everyone. Recognise that you have to satisfy the needs of your children first and foremost, and go on from there to deal with yourself, and everyone else. Don't become charged up by the demands of family and friends who suddenly 'cannot live' without the presence of your children at their gathering. And don't let yourself and your divorce become the focus of all the other tensions and conflict that may be brewing in the rest of the family group. Try to be as reasonable, flexible, and co-operative as possible, to both your ex- and to your children. This is the only way the situation can end up being tolerable, let alone satisfying, for your children. Sit down with the other parent and plan the occasion *well ahead of time.* Here are some of the key questions you should resolve: Do both parents attend? Who brings the children? Do the parents sit in different areas? Near each other? Are both parents involved – and to what degree – in the planning of the occasion? (An example would be your child's birthday party. Which parent buys the cake, sends out the invitations, organises the games, makes the sandwiches for your child's guests . . . and which parent just shows up and says hello? Or do both parents share the work? Are there costs involved? Who pays? How are the costs divided?)

If members of both families are invited or expected to be

there (aunts, uncles, grandparents), how will each of you handle the members of your respective families, who may not know
how to behave in such a situation? Should you inform some of
them that your ex-spouse will also be there? Should you make a
point of steering each other toward – or away from – certain
family members? Should you 'get your stories straight' about
what you may have said, or not said, about the divorce to
certain members of each other's family?

Recognise the importance of close, sensitive discussion with
the children themselves. If possible, test your plans with the
children beforehand, and get their reaction. How will they feel
if they arrive with Mummy, and go home with Daddy? How
will they feel about sitting with Grandma and Grandpa, in
order to avoid embarrassing Mummy and Daddy? *Get their
input.* Don't use this as another excuse for a tug-of-war, with the
children as the prize.

Now let's look at a few specific situations.

Religious holidays and ceremonies If religion matters to both
parents, each of whom wishes the children to profit from the
'extra closeness' of a religious festival, then special arrangements will be needed so that that children can share such times
with both of you.

One simple solution is to have alternate years for different
holidays: Christmas with one parent, Easter with the other,
and the reverse next year. In some faiths, many holidays have
two or more days of observance and celebration, and these may
be split: in a Jewish family, for example, the child may spend
the first day of Rosh Hashanah with one parent, the second day
with the other parent.

If you are not particularly interested in religion, and your
ex-spouse is, let the children spend some extra time with this
parent during the important religious holidays.

Never laugh at or condemn the other parent's religious beliefs (if different from your own). If you do differ on religious
practice, it is perfectly all right to point out or discuss the
differences with the children, assuming they are old enough,
and to point out that in time the children will be able to choose
and set their own level of religious belief and practice.

During the time you are with the children, do not encourage them to break religious laws or customs that may be important to them, or to the other parent. This does not mean the other parent should impose *new* requirements on the children. But if the children were already saying their prayers at bedtime, or observing dietary laws, do no encourage them to break this habit when they are with you.

If the children are old enough to give responsible answers, by all means ask them where they would choose to spend their religious holidays. Respect their answers, and try to accommodate them.

If you are the more religious parent, never act in a 'holier than thou' manner. Respect the other parent's belief (or non-belief). Do not hide what you yourself believe, and be willing to discuss your beliefs openly and honestly with the children, if they are old enough to understand. But don't pass judgement on the other parent.

Holidays Christmas holidays, Easter, summer holidays – all vacation periods should be planned *well in advance*.

Arrange where the children will be during each holiday.

Schedule things so that the children do, indeed, have a holiday, and are not spending all their time in a shuttle from one parent to the other.

Recognise that because of different financial situations, and possibly different opportunities for each parent to get away on holiday, the possibilities open to children may also be quite different between one parent and the other. You may be able to take the children away to a resort for a few weeks; your ex- may only be able to go on excursions in the city. This does not mean that one form of holiday is 'better' than the other!

Don't try to buy your children's affection with exorbitant, exotic holiday plans. Remember the 'acid test' I asked you to apply to regular visits when you are tempted to plan entertainment or special events: is it something that would have been natural and appropriate *before* you were separated?

Try to co-ordinate with your ex- both the type of holiday and the timing, so that your children can benefit from both without a conflict of interest.

Get some input from the children – particularly if they are a
little older – as to what type of experiences would be most
interesting and useful to them. After all, it is *their* vacation.
Sometimes getting a summer job may be better for them than a
long trip somewhere with you.

Birthdays Children in all families know that although their
birthday is a very special day, the actual birthday party is
usually held at a time convenient to parents, school, friends –
often as much as a week or so on either side of the birth date
itself.

Because children usually do not worry if the celebration does
not take place on the exact birthday, you have some built-in
flexibility with which to work, and your child will likely accept
whatever arrangements you work out. The child could have a
birthday party in the home, for school-friends, supervised by
the custodial parent. If possible, the outside parent could be
invited to attend. But if not possible, there is no need to get into
a struggle – simply have another party or 'celebration' of some
kind with the other parent, on the next visit.

Regardless of the visiting parent's attendance at, or absence
from the 'in-house' birthday celebrations, cards and phone
calls on the special day can make the absent parent much more
visible and important in the child's mind.

Keep things simple! There is no reason for birthdays to be the
flashpoint they so often are. Recognise that the child will accept
separate celebrations, or some flexibility in arrangements.
There is no need to change the usual party. Since he will not
make a fuss, why should you? Recognise the impact of a simple
little thing like a phone call.

What happens, though, if the birthday we are talking about
is your own? Or the other parent's? Again, there should be no
problem, if you relax about it and do not try to over-complicate
things. If you are the visiting parent, be prepared to alter your
access arrangements to allow the children to share in a birthday celebration for the other parent, particularly where that
other parent's family may be involved. And the same holds
true in the other direction: if you are the custodial parent, be
prepared to allow for a visit that does not fall into the normal

scheduling, so that the children can share the visiting parent's birthday.

In both cases, your children will usually love to show you their gifts for the other parent, birthday cards they have made all by themselves, etc. Allow them to have this 'show and tell', and be enthusiastic (all right, so maybe it is hard!) in sharing their happiness and satisfaction.

Illness When the child gets ill, no matter how mild the illness is or how short its duration, there may be some regressive behaviour. At the same time, the parents tend to feel helpless, and the normal guilt feelings about the divorce can become literally massive.

A lot of this turbulence will, of course, disappear when the child recovers. So you cannot 'cure' all of the emotional upsets by anything you do, or do not do.

But you can make things worse. There are some important points to be aware of.

First, do not blame the other parent for not looking after the child well enough. (I am assuming that we are not dealing with illness arising out of severe child abuse, criminal negligence, etc. If you do have some concerns about the other parent's attention to the child's health, and those concerns appear valid to you, save them until the child gets better, and then raise them in a positive, constructive, 'what can we both do to prevent this in the future' atmosphere.)

Second, be willing to alter visiting arrangements for the child's own good. This could mean compromises in both directions. For example, if you are the visiting parent, you should be prepared to forgo taking the child out of the house if the child is too ill. Do not insist that it is *your* visiting day, and the child *must* come with you.

On the other hand, if you are the custodial parent, you also must be ready to compromise. If the child is able to leave the house – but is still ill enough to require attention, medication, etc. – there is no reason why the visit cannot take place and the other parent do the caring. If in doubt, consult the child's doctor.

Another compromise required of the custodial parent is the

good sense to invite the other parent to visit the child *in the home*. If at all possible, let the other parent be alone in the home with the child. Be sure to tell the child that *this is only a visit*, and that the child's illness will not cause the parents to re-unite.

Finally, both of you must be sure to communicate, not just during the course of the illness, but afterwards. How did the illness start? Was it something that both of you should be on the look-out for, from now on? (And I am not necessarily talking about something major, or complicated: it can be as simple as, 'This flu is all over town, and the doctors says that even though he's better, he has to wear a sweater every time he's outside.') How did the child respond to treatment? Should he be taking regular medication? Should you be watching for a reaction? Did you notice anything that seems to contradict what the other parent, or even the doctor, expected? *Share all information*.

And don't let your child's illness become an excuse for more guilt about your divorce. Kids become ill with or without a divorce.

Out of school activities Sports, dancing, music lessons and other extra-curricular activities are important for children, and should be planned with parental visits in mind. These activities give *both* parents the chance to share in the child's progress, and it is important for the child to be able to display new skills, accomplishments, or big moments in life, to *both* parents. Careful planning should eliminate all problems. If possible, aim to have both of you there for all 'big events' – there is usually enough of a crowd, and enough attention focused on the event (and not on you) for you both to be in attendance, even if you are sitting in different sections of the audience.

CHAPTER 6

School

Most children enjoy school. Most children also take part in, and enjoy, various extra-curricular activities. They like learning, doing, taking on challenges, having a sense of accomplishment. And a big part of their satisfaction is the sharing of these experiences – both the successes and the failures – with adults who are important to them.

That means you, of course.

But it also means teachers, coaches, youth leaders, and in fact any adults who are involved in the child's educational, athletic, social or cultural activities. Your children have relationships with these adults. Your children have relationships with these adults' environments – school, club, gym, community centre. And just as your divorce may throw a strain on your children's relationship with you, so it may throw a strain on their relationship with these other important adults, and with the outside environment they represent.

If this happens, you can expect certain behavioural and other problems. As a responsible parent, you should know the typical problems to watch for, how and why they occur, and what to do about them.

Let's begin by studying an actual case.

Billy, Sarah and Mike are three children in the same family. Their parents are divorced. Their mother has custody, and their father has regular access. The custodial arrangement was worked out very amicably. While the children had experienced some of the normal adjustment problems to the separation and subsequent divorce, the fact that the divorce process itself was a peaceful and co-operative one made the parents both surprised and perplexed when each of the three children began to demonstrate some serious problems with school.

Billy, aged six, was in the Infants School. One day he decided he was not going to go to school for a while. First, he complained of headaches and a sore throat. When this ruse had run its course, he said he simply did not want to go. He would cry and become extremely anxious when his mother insisted. While at school, he would not participate in class. Instead, he kept asking the teacher to let him go home. This attitude towards school attendance was entirely out of character.

Sarah, nine, at primary school, also displayed a dramatic change in behaviour patterns. Previously, she had been a friendly, outgoing girl. An average student, she had never been unusually keen on schoolwork, and while her marks were always satisfactory, she had never particularly applied herself with exceptional diligence. Now she became extremely concerned with being at school punctually. She became rigid about following every single rule. She became very involved in schoolwork, to a point that could have been described as obsessive, in comparison to her previous attitude. But she also became completely unsociable. She would not go to school early or stay late to play with friends. She gave up all out-of-school activities, and came straight home the minute school ended, so that she could 'help mother'.

Mike, fourteen, was at secondary school and had never been a discipline problem. Now he began to be rebellious, both at school and at home. This rebelliousness went far beyond the normal stage of 'feeling their oats' that is typical of early teenagers. Mike started acting the 'tough guy' role. He mouthed off to his teachers. He bragged about being heavily into drugs (he confided to me that he was really 'not doing anything heavier than pot').

So here we have three children from the same family, each at a different stage of development, reacting differently but with many similarities, to their parents' divorce. We can compare their situation to that of a family infected by a virus. The adults have the sniffles, runny noses and a general malaise. The oldest child has laryngitis; the middle child has bronchitis; the baby has pneumonia. Biologically, we would be dealing with the same organism, the same system, being attacked; but there are different reactions to the attack, different levels of danger to the patient, different therapeutic steps, and different recuperation times.

What were these problems all about? Why did they occur? Why did they take the form they did?

It took several sessions before I could get Billy, the youngest, to open up. His fear turned out to be a typical one: being 'found out' at school.

Billy loved his teacher, but was now afraid that if she found out that 'Daddy left Mummy', she would be angry with Billy himself. Perhaps she would shame him by making an example of him during a 'Show and Tell' session. Billy envisioned the teacher saying, 'I have some special news for the class today. Do you know what's happened to Billy's Daddy? He left Billy's Mummy. Now, class, can you all tell Billy what you think of that?' Maybe his teacher would tell the principal! Maybe Billy would have to move away from the school. He remembered something like that happening to another boy, Mark, who had suddenly disappeared from class one day. Later, someone had told Billy that Mark had had to move far away because his parents were getting a divorce. At the time, Billy did not even know what the word meant. Now he knew for sure.

Billy was also worried about his schoolmates' reaction. Would they call him 'cry-baby' and not let him play football with them anymore? Would he be shunned?

I was able to help Billy understand that teachers know all about divorce, and understand how kids feel when their parents get a divorce. I told him that teachers are ready and eager to help children talk about it whenever the children themselves are ready. I assured him that his teacher would never tell anybody else, but would leave it to Billy to announce and explain things in his own good time.

With some prompting and encouragement from me, Billy finally decided to talk to his teacher alone, before going back to school. This sensitive teacher told Billy that she had missed him. In fact, the whole class had missed him, was worried about him and wanted him back among them. This sense of being wanted (coupled with relief that he would *not* be singled out and shamed, would not even have to talk about the divorce if he did not want to) was all that Billy needed. He returned to the classroom and the pleasure he had formerly experienced at school took over again. Billy was soon back to his old self – at school and at home.

Sarah's story was different. Her problem, it developed, stemmed from a feeling that her mother was being overburdened by having been left alone. Sarah felt that she should help out more, that she would now have to do much more in the house. Playtime before and after school was rationalised away, as being 'silly kid's stuff anyway'. On the other hand, the schoolwork itself was 'real work' and so it became extremely important for Sarah to do well. Of course, Sarah was alienating her friends, who could not understand why she had suddenly become a 'holier than thou' student with no room for the normal frivolities of the typical nine-year-old.

Sarah confided that her being more 'adult' might make her be more appreciated by her 'sad' mother. She did not want to 'be a baby' and overburden her mother even further. A little more work with Sarah revealed another, deeper reason for her to want to discard the 'child' role and identity: being a child left her vulnerable to adults (parents) who argue and separate. Being an 'adult' would lessen this vulnerability.

It was essential that Sarah's mother should involve herself in the solution to Sarah's problem. With some of the understanding gained from my sessions with Sarah, her mother was able to tell the youngster that she appreciated her help, was pleased by her good marks, but was worried about Sarah missing out on 'the fun things which are so important'. Her mother also made it clear to Sarah that being an 'adult' was no protection against vulnerability. She told Sarah that adults, too, suffer from a divorce; that she, the mother, was suffering, but would overcome her suffering by allowing herself to enjoy certain activities. Sarah should, too.

This message helped considerably, but it was necessary to turn it into positive action. The mother encouraged Sarah to invite a former friend over to play. The visit was an enjoyable one, and Sarah's outlook began to brighten. The mother encouraged repeat visits, and then visits with more and more friends. Sarah's birthday was coming up, and the mother threw herself into planning the party along with Sarah. She became more and more involved in Sarah's needs, not only pleasing the child, but also demonstrating that she, the mother, was not quite the weak and overburdened person who desperately needed Sarah's 'adult'-like help. Soon Sarah was back to her usual self – bright, cheerful, gregarious.

I chose not to involve Sarah's father directly in solving Sarah's problem, since a big part of that problem stemmed from Sarah's interpretation of the plight of the custodial parent, the mother. But the father was kept fully informed of all that was going on.

Sarah's image of her overburdened mother was a main component of her problem, but not the only one. I have already mentioned another cause: her desire to assume an 'adult' identity so as to reduce her vulnerability to other adults – who, as she had learned, can fight and separate. But there was a third factor, which I did not learn about until almost a year later, when Sarah revealed it to her father: during that 'bad period', she told him, one of the reasons she always wanted to come straight home from school was her fear that her father might come along and 'kidnap' her.

Now let's turn to Mike, the fourteen-year-old. His behaviour pattern was the most aggressive and anti-social of the three children: rebellious, pretending to be tough, being very rude to his teachers, skipping classes, exaggerating his usage of drugs.

Mike, it turned out, was also very worried about the divorce. He was worried about his status with his peers. He feared that his parents' divorce might point him out to them as 'different' – weak, damaged, less masculine. That he could worry about being considered 'different' showed that Mike was having trouble accepting himself. Being 'tough' is a common response, at this age, to problems of self-identity.

Even before I examined Mike's problems, there were some encouraging signs. For one thing, he had not yet followed the route of serious drug abuse. He was only pretending to have done so. This meant he was eyeing it as a possibility, as being the 'cool' thing to do, something that his friends would admire. That he had thus far restrained himself from actually doing it, though, was a good omen.

Another positive sign was that Mike seemed very touched by the fact that his sister and brother were having problems of their own. He was eager to help them deal with these problems. In fact, he had offered a lot of encouragement to both Billy and Sarah, fulfilling the 'big brother' role in a healthy and constructive way.

Eventually, Mike agreed to see me alone. Maybe I could help, just as he, the elder brother, had helped his younger siblings. As Mike gradually opened up to me, it became clear that his problems involved much more than compensating for a lack of self-esteem caused by the divorce.

Mike told me that he was very worried about his mother. She was so attractive: what was she going to do sexually? He did not want his teachers to become too friendly with her. Maybe one of them would try to make advances. That, he explained, was the main reason he was constantly fighting his teachers.

I suggested to Mike that, paradoxically, his behaviour was bringing about the very situation he was trying to prevent: his mother was being drawn into closer contact with his teachers, to discuss his recurring discipline problems. Was it not possible, I suggested, that his *real* wish, underneath it all, was to bring Mum and the teachers together?

After some shrill protests, and claims that I was 'crazy', Mike thought about it, and did see some discrepancy between what he claimed to want to do and what he in fact was doing.

We finally concluded that in the same way that he did not want his mother to run his life (this feeling becoming very strong in *all* children at this age), so he could not run hers. There would be a mutual respect, a mutual feeling of responsibility. But it was not up to Mike to control his mother. Mike came to realise that he would have to deal with the fact that his mother still had sexual needs and that these needs were her business to handle.

Mike's problems were essentially caused by some normal developmental stages becoming tangled up with the impact of the divorce. The typical fourteen-year-old desire for independence, and concern with peer pressure – which often displays itself in an exaggerated 'adult' pose – became acute when the divorce gave Mike even more good reasons to worry about his 'image'. The 'tough guy' became a means of securing that image.

It took a lot of hard work, patience, and talking, to get Mike to understand the source of the problem. Once he had the insight, though, the problem disappeared almost immediately.

The cases of Billy, Sarah and Mike illustrate some of the typical problems children can encounter – or more correctly, create – at school or at other activities outside the home, as a result of their parents' divorce and their reaction to it. While the details of the child's actual behaviour or misbehaviour will vary from case to case, we see the same major *causes* cropping up again and again.

1. Fear of being considered different

The child fears that his parents' divorce will cause teachers, coaches, and peers, to look at him as 'different', or 'not as good'. One response is to avoid the situation that will confirm the validity of the fear; thus we have 'illnesses' to keep the child away from school, or direct pleas to be allowed to stay home – or, finally, truancy. Another response is gradually to slip into chronic (mis)behaviour that affirms the child's low opinion of himself.

2. A need for control

The divorce proved to the child, with devastating impact, that he had little or no control over his world. The parents he had counted on, the stable home environment he had assumed was always going to be there, disappeared ... and nothing he could say or do could prevent this. Many children react to this dramatic proof of their own impotence by seeking to create some new situation in which they *can* exert some control. Misbehaving accomplished that objective. The consequences may be unpleasant – punishment – but at least the child is in control, and the adults are responding to *him*. Another way of exerting some control is to take on an adult-like role, as with Sarah's compulsive need to 'help' her mother ('Look, I'm grown up now') and to put some distance between herself and her friends ('I'm a grown-up now, not like you'). The child needs to compensate for the powerlessness she felt throughout the divorce process.

3. Sheer exhaustion

This last point may sound rather down-to-earth, but do not underrate its importance. The child, having poured so much emotional (and sometimes, physical) energy into coping with the separation and divorce now has less energy with which to handle the normal day-to-day challenges of school or extra-curricular activities. This can lead to mistakes, failures, which in turn can create a variety of problems. The child can conclude that he really is no good, that there is no point in trying, confusing his failure to prevent the divorce ('It was my fault, it happened because I was bad') and his failure in school ('See, that proves I'm no good'). Or the child can look to create a 'success' by becoming the centre of attention through negative behaviour.

To an extent, there is little you can do to prevent these problems. But the degree to which a serious problem develops, or its duration if it does develop, is very much subject to your response to it. Let us review some of the major steps you can, and should, take.

If you are the custodial parent, then be sure to keep the outside parent fully informed as to the children's school and extra-curricular activities. Provide copies of school sports and club schedules, special announcements of impending events, etc. What you are after here is constant communication that helps the other parent become attuned to normal everyday school and out-of-school activites. With such knowledge, the other parent can do a much more effective job of supporting you as you cope with the child's problem. If the other parent is out of touch, or uninformed, it is much more difficult for you to receive effective support.

Consult your children's teachers, coaches, etc., *before* any problems develop. Explain your marital situation to them. It is not necessary to go into all the details. Just let them know that your children's education is very important to you, and that you do not want your divorce to disrupt it and cause problems for your children. You are not really asking them for anything at this stage, you are just 'letting them know'. These days, most educators and youth leaders are only too aware of children struggling to cope with a divorce. They will know what signs to look for, and they will co-operate by giving you early warning of any problem.

If they do not show any interest in helping you, and try to tell you that 'your divorce is *your* problem, not ours', confront them. Tell them that this attitude is almost certain to be harmful to your children. If they still fail to show a co-operative attitude, go over their heads. And if you do not get a positive response at this level, then I would seriously consider withdrawing your child from that particular school or group.

Involve your ex- when you talk to your children's teachers. If you are consulting with them in the absence of the outside parent, then be sure to tell them that they can expect to hear from that parent from time to time, and that you would like them to co-operate with both of you. They will probably welcome this information, as it takes a lot of pressure off them, eliminating the need to second-guess themselves about what it is safe to say to one parent and not to the other. All the political manœuvring is eliminated, and everyone can do what is right for the children. Your readiness to co-operate with the other parent provides an incentive and an encouragement to the teachers, coaches etc., to be co-operative, too. Even better than *telling* them about the other parent's involvement is getting your ex-spouse to accompany you. This is an even more dramatic demonstration to them of how important your children's welfare is to both of you: although divorced, here you are together to discuss your children with their teachers. It sets up a very healthy, positive climate which can only benefit the children.

The above steps will, in many cases, provide an effective 'early warning system' to nip problems in the bud. And even if the problems become severe, you at least have a structure of teamwork, co-operation, and communication, so that the problem can be attacked much more quickly and effectively.

Boarding School. When children go away to boarding school, they often encounter feelings of homesickness. To help alleviate this, there are opportunities for parents to visit and exeats for the children, usually for half-term, sometimes just for the day. The parents arrive at the school often laden with sweets and other treats, and the children rush to greet them. Parents and children spend the day together and the children have a chance to catch up on news from home and re-establish bonds with their loved ones, while at the same time sharing with the parents all the wonderful things that are happening at school. By the end of the week-end the children are usually quite ready to go back to school, or if it is a day exeat, for their parents to go back home! But the visit has diluted the feelings of homesickness, and enabled the children to resume their school life. These exeats and parents' visiting days can be quite hard on the children of a divorced couple. They may worry about having to tell their friends about the situation. They may worry about having to 'present' their parents to their teachers one at a time, and at different periods of the day. But most of all, they worry about having to face, yet again, the conflict between their parents. They can handle all of these pressures, though, if the *parents* behave properly during the visit, and if the children are not tugged at, pulled apart, competed for.

If the two of you still get along well enough to carry out the visit together, then that is obviously the ideal arrangement. You may, of course, want to arrive at the school separately, but time your arrival so that, in effect, you can carry out the visit substantially the same way as any other set of parents. But if this is not possible, then you will have to do some careful planning. *Make sure the plans are specific – and don't pull any surprises on the other parent.* Familiarise yourself with the school's expectations about arrival and departure times, flexibility about rules, and past experiences with similar situations. Whatever else you do, *don't* make the children feel that it is up to them to make *you* happy – it is their half-term or day out. Let them show you around the school, talk to you about their accomplishments, adventures, problems. Concentrate on sharing with them their school experience, rather than worrying about the logistics of the visit itself (like who is fetching them or taking them back, who is eating lunch with who, etc). These logistics should be worked out as part of your advanced planning – and the children should never be involved in having to make a choice between the two of you. This just adds a lot of unnecessary pressure. If you cannot work things out so that both of you are there on the same day, you may have to trade one half-term or exeat for another. This would be no problem if there are enough during the school year. But if not, you would have to take one half-term and the other parent take the next. This may sound drastic, but as far as I am concerned the absolute priority is the children's enjoyment of a (relatively) pressure-free half-term or exeat, and if the two of you cannot even work out some peaceful arrangements in advance, then the chances are that there will be some conflict erupting during the half-term or exeat itself, to the serious detriment of the children.

Now let's look at your relationship with the children themselves.

It is likely that your child will express some fears that your divorce will cause him to be treated differently at school. If this happens, *do not belittle or dismiss the child's fears as being groundless*. It is much better to have these fears expressed openly, than to keep them bottled up. Tell the child that you can understand his concern, that it is only natural to wonder about the reaction from the teachers and the other kids at school. But you can also offer some very strong reassurances:

1. Explain that the child will not automatically be condemned, isolated or victimised unless he reacts to his own fears by behaving in such a way as to bring about negative attention from his teachers and schoolmates.
2. Explain that you have already talked to the teachers, and that they have assured you they will be understanding and supportive. The child will also be relieved to learn that the teachers will be on the look-out for negative or unfair conduct by the other kids at school.
3. Explain that the other parent has also been involved in this consultation with the school, and that both of you are ready and willing to co-operate in every way.

It is possible, of course, that your child is at an age when he prefers to handle this on his own. If that is the case, do not try to squeeze his fears and anxieties out of him. Be open and ready to discuss the problem if *he* raises it, but do not try to force the pace yourself.

Make sure that the custodial/access arrangements do not disrupt the children's normal school and extra-curricular activities. When a boy has to give up his regular weekly football game, or a girl her dancing class, because that is the time that Dad comes for his visit, the children are not only disappointed, but are also learning that the divorce really does interfere with their legitimate needs. This needlessly accentuates the negative impact of the divorce. Let the children know that their needs will be respected above any other plans which the custodial or visiting parent may have for that time. *Yes, it may be hard for you!* Sometimes, it will require a great deal of flexibility, but it is a necessity.

Just as custodial/access arrangements should not disrupt out-of-school activities, so should they not interrupt homework, studying for exams, and the 'work' (as opposed to 'recreation') side of the child's life. Visits are not holidays from the child's regular responsibilities. The children can just as easily take their homework with them.

Make sure *both of you* provide positive reinforcement for the children's accomplishments. When your children bring home essays, projects, term papers, etc., with good results – or good exam results – of course you should demonstrate your pride and pleasure. But don't stop there. Tell them you are sure their other parent will be just as excited. Encourage them to show the report or project to that parent.

When a child brings home results that are not quite as good, deal with the problem the way you normally would have done before the divorce. You will know whether it calls for a mild scolding or a 'heavy' discussion. And again, make sure you let the other parent know, so that your responses are alike. Remember what I said in the very first chapter: the child needs you as a *parent* in spite of the divorce; such a relationship includes both parental pleasure and parental reproof, and the child will be quite comfortable with both. Both reactions can be demonstrated even when the parents are living apart, provided the two of you consult and co-operate.

Sometimes, a child will ask you *not* to share 'bad news' with the other parent. What then? Frankly, it *is* a touchy and difficult question. Occasionally, but only very occasionally, should you respect the child's wishes. The acid test should be: would you have kept the information from this parent if you were still married? If you decide to respect your child's wishes, be sure to discuss your decision fully with the child, letting it be clearly understood that you do not approve of keeping something like this from the other parent, even though you are willing to go along with it just this once.

At the same time, however, encourage the child to work the problem through with the outside parent. Offer your help. If the child tells you he is afraid of dealing with the other parent on this particular issue (perhaps because of a real or imagined bias on the part of the other parent), express sympathy for the child *but do not condemn the other parent.*

The above steps are largely preventive. Their objective is to establish a 'normal' operating environment for a child, one which assures him that his school and out-of-school activities can proceed on schedule and that the divorce need not get in the way; one which shows him that he has the same responsibilities as he did before the divorce; and one which gives him the opportunity to enjoy contact with both parents in the same way as he did *before* the divorce, sharing good reports and failed exams alike, seeing both of them cheering him on at cricket or hearing good reports from his teacher or coach. This climate of 'normality' reduces the child's fear that the divorce will somehow set him apart from his teachers, coaches, peers. The fear may be there at the outset, but as the evidence mounts on the positive side, as the child sees, week-in and week-out, that the same activities carry on as usual, that the same duties and responsibilities exist as before, that his parents are involved in school and out-of-school activities in the same way, the child will gradually feel more and more secure, and will not be able to blame the divorce for destroying the old familiar patterns. As the child gains confidence in the continuity of these familiar patterns, he loses many of the reasons that would otherwise contribute to behaviour problems.

Finally, if in spite of all of these preventive measures, you still encounter severe behaviour problems or other kinds of adjustment problems, do not hesitate to seek professional advice. The school, if properly informed and consulted, should be able to help, and you should listen carefully to what the teachers have to say. Your child may require therapy for further guidance.

Do not attempt to carry the entire burden yourself. As I have tried to indicate in this chapter, there are many steps you can and should take to head off problems before they occur. But you may also reach the point at which it is necessary to have professional help. It is important to your child's welfare, and your own, that you seek such help promptly.

CHAPTER 7

Your New Life

Up to this point, we have been doing a lot of talking about keeping things the same as they were before, as far as your children are concerned. The same parenting relationship, even if the structure has changed. The same standards of discipline. The same environment at school, with friends, with out-of-school activities. The same household chores. The same rules for bedtime, watching TV, doing homework. Love, time spent together, discipline, supervision – these are all aspects of the parent–child relationship, and I have stressed how important it is to show the children that the divorce need not undermine the integrity of this relationship.

But of course, many things do *not* stay the same. And one of the most important changes that can influence your children is the change that takes place in *your life* as an adult. You are now 'free'.

You have the opportunity to enter into new relationships. One of them may culminate in another marriage. How do you handle this? What problems can it cause with your children – and how do you deal with them? Where do your own 'rights' as an adult conflict with your responsibilities as a parent – and how do you reconcile the conflict? These are some of the issues I will deal with in this chapter.

First, let us understand that there are several different ways in which your 'post-divorce' life can change.

Actual new freedom You are no longer inhibited by the demands and conflicts imposed by your ex-spouse (or even by your ex-spouse's family). Your life used to revolve around these conflicts. Now it does not.

Imagined new freedom In reality, you had the freedom to do things before, but you blamed your ex-spouse for not allowing you to do them.

Feeling lost You are alone, and you feel lonely. You are not thinking about 'freedom', and about all the wonderful things you can now do. Your focus is on losing somebody (even if that somebody was a source of trouble to you). You are not used to being alone. You do not want to be alone. (This feeling of loneliness is the most common reason cited by those who, following a divorce, head almost immediately into another relationship – which often results in a new marriage).

Feeling hurt Even in those marriages where there is a great deal of anger, even hate, and all love seems to have been lost, I have often seen in both parties a feeling of being hurt by the divorce. Where the marriage was a bitter experience, you would expect to encounter feelings of relief that it is finally over, but it is striking how often this feeling of hurt, of having lost something, is expressed.

There are important reasons for this. We must go back to the time of the marriage itself. Most people marry someone whom they feel they love, and who loves them. This produces feelings of euphoria, of well-being, of safety, of caring for and being cared for. Such feelings are akin to the feelings we experience early in our lives, in relation to our parents – feelings of security, of love from and for a loved one. Such feelings rank among the strongest passions we experience.

Loss of these feelings produces equally strong feelings of hurt and rejection. Thus, where our *rational* response to a terrible marriage might be, 'I'm glad I'm finally rid of that terrible relationship', what in fact happens is that our *emotions*, these feelings of hurt and rejection, overwhelm us and produce a very different reaction: 'I have been rejected. I have been hurt.' And the reasons for the rejection usually centre on the self: 'I'm no good', 'I am unlovable', 'I am sexually inadequate'.

Such feelings of hurt and rejection quickly translate into a follow-up reaction: 'I've got to find someone else.' Your self-esteem has been battered, and there is the natural desire immediately to try to regain that self-esteem by proving your worthiness in another relationship. Often, this will result in behaviour quite untypical of your former self. I have seen many people over-react to their hurt by putting on a mask that shows the world they are *not* hurt, they were *not* rejected.

They become the 'bon vivant', they parade an active, overt sex life into which they try to project as much glamour and excitement as possible. What they are really doing is talking to themselves, and what they are saying is: 'You see? You weren't really rejected. You weren't really unlovable. You weren't really sexually unattractive or inadequate. Look at all the action you've got now! Doesn't that prove it?'

You can go on like this for a while – but in the end you still have to deal with yourself. That is why it is better not to react while you are still feeling hurt. Give yourself time to recuperate on your own, or with old friends whose caring and patience you can depend on. In the short term, it may be a bit tougher to live with your feelings of hurt and rejection. But there is a bigger danger in not being real, in trying to pretend. It makes you vulnerable to people who are all too ready and willing to take advantage of you. And the next crash, when it comes, will be that much more devastating.

It is also harmful for your children.

Remember that they, too, have been hurt by the separation and divorce. As we have seen, they often feel responsible for the marital split. One parent has left (rejected) them; will the other parent leave too? Their self-esteem may be as battered as yours. You feel unsuccessful and rejected as a husband or wife; they feel rejected as people. Depending on their age and stage of development, they may blame everything on the behaviour they were displaying around the time of the separation, not understanding that it was normal and typical of their current stage of physical and emotional growth. *They need your support.* Even if you are depressed, they need you and your assurance that you are still available to them, aware of their hurt, aware of their emotional struggles. If, instead of giving them this support, you get involved in the escape I have described above, you are doing a disservice both to yourself and to your children.

So what do you do? Not go on living? Not go out with someone new? Not pursue that career you have always wanted? Stay home forever and just keep soothing the children's hurt feelings?

Of course not. You have to go on living. You need, and are

entitled to, your own identity as an adult, and this means enjoying the full range of self-expression, from social to sexual to professional. There are just two important riders:

Be aware of the escaping problems I have described.

Be aware of your responsibilities to your children.

Let's examine this second issue.

New Relationships and Sexuality

Don't be afraid to talk with your children about the fact that you will be going out with people of the opposite sex. Depending on the children's age and maturity, they will have many questions about this. Listen to their questions and be as tolerant of their concerns as you possibly can. Be as frank as possible, based on your judgement of their understanding and maturity.

Regardless of the specific questions your children ask, remember that their underlying question is: 'How much do I stand to lose from all this?' They are worried that if you find someone else, you may decide that the children are superfluous, unneeded, unwanted. They may react to your going out with someone new by asking questions, directly or indirectly. They may not ask any questions at all, but instead act out their anxieties by misbehaving, developing a rash, cough or other illness (to return your attention to them), or displaying other forms of regressive behaviour. Be sensitive to, and aware of this. If you can connect their behaviour to this anxiety, do so and bring it out into the open and talk about it with them.

Always act in a way that is reassuring. If you have a date, tell the children ahead of time, and handle any protest calmly but firmly. Do not sneak up on them and give them the news at the last second, or deceive them in some other way.

Be honest in explaining your needs. This does not mean you have to go into unnecessary detail. Simply explain that you intend to go out, and will do so, because other adults are important in your life. Stress that it is *not because you are dissatisfied with the children*. It is just that you need adult company in addition to theirs, in the same way that they themselves need relationships with friends of their own age in addition to their relationship with you. This is something they can understand. They have needs – so do you. It does not mean you intend to neglect the children.

When you meet someone new and exciting, it is only natural to want to spend most of your time with them. That is probably how it was when you were single, and first met your ex-spouse. Once you start going out again, you may be fortunate enough to meet someone special, and you may then experience again that feeling of excitement, of wanting to be with this person all the time.

But there is a difference now: you are responsible for your children, too, and you will therefore have to adapt your activities to take into account your children's real needs. Therefore, part of your evaluation of your 'new friend' will have to include the friend's potential relationship with your children.

Does this person enjoy children? Share and understand your involvement with your children? Tolerate your co-operation with your ex-spouse, in dealing with the children? Or is your new friend likely to complicate the struggle between you and your ex-spouse?

I have seen it work both ways. In some cases, finding a new partner has helped to ease the custody and access struggle between the parents. Unfortunately, I have seen an equal number of cases in which the new friend could not tolerate the presence of the ex-spouse, and pushed and challenged the ex-spouse into further fights, and even further legal action. Since the presence of the ex-spouse is usually associated with the children, you can understand how sensitive an area this can be for them.

You also have to look at the new friend's family. Are there children? Are they the same age as your children? Different age? How would the two families fit together? Would they be able to get along with each other? What problems can be expected? For example, would there be major new challenges for your oldest or youngest child? New forms of sibling rivalry? Differences in background that could cause conflicts over values, discipline, responsibilities, level of maturity or soph-istication? Sexual involvement is often an issue. Are there adolescents involved, to whom the families' contact could mean a real struggle of sexuality and morality? How do you all live together?

These issues have to be reviewed quite early in the dating process, as soon as you begin to suspect that you may be heading towards a serious relationship. By focusing on these issues, discussing them, devising strategies to deal with them, you will avoid further needless hurt to yourself, your new friend, and both sets of children. Whatever else you do, *don't* brush these issues away with the vague hope that your new-found 'love' will somehow take care of it!

If the new relationship results in remarriage, Chapter 10 offers further advice on helping your children make the adjustment.

The Parent Without Custody

If you are the parent who does not have custody of children, you face a somewhat different situation, although my early observations about loss, hurt, and escaping into a whirlwind of social activity can still apply.

But the big difference between you and the custodial parent is that you have more free time to pursue a new social life. Since the children do not see you all the time, you do not face the same pressures as the custodial parent, in terms of telling the children that you are dating, and answering their questions. This 'extra freedom' must be handled responsibly, however.

Your social life must not be permitted to infringe upon your visits with the children. Since you have relatively infrequent contact with them, it is only fair that you spend most of this time with them, and not out with your new friends. Most people have little or no difficulty accepting this. They have plenty of time for dating during the rest of the week. The question that does arise, however, is when and how to introduce the children to one's friends, particularly when one particular person has emerged as a potential 'new friend'.

As a general rule, it is much better to delay any introductions until you are fairly seriously involved with the new friend. If you are only casually going out with a variety of people, it is very unfair to the children to expose them to each and every date. It stirs up their emotions needlessly and can cause anxiety and confusion. Is this one a potential 'new Mummy'? Or is this one? Or how about this one? What's going on here?

Wait until you are fairly certain there will be a continuing relationship.

On the other hand, you have to make the introduction before you are too seriously committed, in case the chemistry just does not work between this new friend and your children. If the chemistry is bad, you do not have to drop the new friend! But you will certainly need time to work on the relationship, and if you wait until you are practically remarried before introducing the children, you are denying yourself, your friend, and the children this valuable 'breathing space'.

Your children's reactions may be extremely positive, or extremely negative, and may not always have to do with their actual feelings and conflicts from your divorce. For example, they may react very positively because they feel they have to please *you*. At the same time, problems may crop up that indicate they really are not all that pleased. If you see such patterns – misbehaviour, hypochondria, regressive behaviour – you must bring the problem out in the open and discuss it with them sympathetically.

Overt negative reactions, too, may have nothing to do with the new friend, and everything to do with the divorce. Your new friendship may be the final sign, to the children, that you and their other parent are through, once and for all – and this may be hard for them to accept. Another common phenomenon is that the children feel they have to represent the other parent, and bring into play the hostilities and resentments (real or fantasised) of your ex-spouse. A third possibility, also quite common, is that the children feel displaced as your favourites, by this 'new friend'. The children may even have fantasised themselves as replacements for your ex-spouse, and the emotional intensity of your visits with them (made all the more pronounced by their relative infrequency) may have reinforced this fantasy. Now the new friend is there to take their place.

You can see how important it is, then, to allow *time* to work on your behalf, letting the children gradually become comfortable with the new friend, letting them see that the quality of their time with you is not impaired, that you are not 'replacing' them but simply seeking an additional relationship, with an adult, in the same way that they need relationships with other children of their own age. Time is important – but do not rely on it exclusively.

You should also question your children, openly and sympathetically, as to the reasons for any resentment they show towards your new friend. Is their protest realistic? Does it match one of the causes I have listed above? Discuss it with them as frequently, over as long a period, and as sensitively, as you possibly can.

If there are problems that your children should work through with your new friend, encourage them both to do so – and do not get caught in the middle. At the same time, remember that your *are* the common denominator, the person they have in common. This is a most sensitive problem: handle it cautiously and sensitively, but make certain you also allow your children and the new friend to get to know each other so that you are not always the go-between. Try to give them time alone with each other.

If all else fails, you may have to make a choice, which is very difficult. If you choose to join this new friend in a permanent relationship, in the face of continuing hostility from your children, then you will have to explain it to them and deal with their protests. The explanations I suggest in dealing with the issue of going out with someone new will be helpful here: that you need an adult relationship just as the children need relationships with other children; that it does not mean you are rejecting or abandoning them; that your decision is firm, and was not caused by something the children either did or did not do. But no matter how effective you are, you may also have to engage the help of an outside source, preferably someone who is effective in family therapy, and especially in the problems of 'blended' families.

It is also very important to involve the other parent as soon as you feel serious about your new friend. *In no way are you seeking permission from your ex- for this new relationship.* But you *are* seeking support in helping you to deal with the children in this situation. This support can include being extremely helpful in explaining things to the children, fielding their questions, allaying their fears and anxieties – even shifting visiting times to accommodate your new lifestyle. If the ex-spouse is involved in a positive, constructive way, feelings of being left out and hurt are less likely, and therefore the children are less likely to be used as pawns in expressing the other parent's own resentment of your new relationship.

Now let's turn the situation around for a moment.

Suppose it is *your ex-spouse* that has got into a new relationship. Suppose that you do not approve of the new relationship. That it makes you angry ... fearful ... jealous ... bitter ... What then? Can you be expected to help 'sell' it to the children?

If you care about the children, *yes*. You will just have to accept the frustration of not being able to do anything to stop the new relationship. You must not react to it by using your children as an audience for the outpouring of your resentment. Do not question them about your ex-spouse's activities, or the new friend. If you have any legitimate protests, for whatever reason, take them directly to your ex-spouse. If nothing can be done, and your ex-spouse is firm in the resolve to pursue or formalise the new relationship, then involving your children in your unhappiness with the situation will only hurt them, and do nothing to correct the situation itself.

Dealing with Your Sexuality

This last topic applies to both custodial and visiting parents, and to all phases of your new relationships, be they casual or serious. Since some of these relationships may involve sexual activity, you may have some quite natural concerns about how to conceal it from the children, or explain it to them if they ask. To put it simply: be discreet. Handle the issue of your sexual activity in the same way you handled it when you were married. Most probably, it was a natural and healthy part of your life that your children became aware of, and accepted, when they were old enough and mature enough to do so. It should be exactly the same now.

It is difficult to give hard-and-fast rules, because this issue is very much connected with personal standards of morality, and you should definitely not do anything that makes you feel uncomfortable. If you have a new romance – and if that new partner has been gradually introduced to the children in the ways that have been described earlier in this chapter – then I see nothing wrong with continuing to share room and bed with that partner even when the children are there, providing this is compatible with your moral or religious beliefs. I would, however, avoid sharing room and bed in the presence of the children if the relationship is only casual or in the very early stages.

Unfortunately, though, some people have a tendency to flaunt their new sexual exploits in front of their children and their ex-spouse, in order to 'hurt' the latter. (They may be quite happy to let the children know about it, if this means the children will serve as a means of informing the ex-spouse.) The tactic may be successful, and may indeed hurt the ex-spouse, but it is also likely to hurt and confuse the children, who probably have no frame of reference with which to understand or cope with this new information. As well, it will further alienate the ex-spouse, often triggering further destructive behaviour through the children.

What about sex *with* your ex-spouse? Believe it or not, this is quite common. Often while co-operating in taking the children back and forth, in discussing the children, you may find yourself experiencing quite tender feelings towards your ex-. As you watch the good, more sensitive side of the 'other parent' at work, the old feelings return and you soon find yourselves in bed. Morally there is nothing wrong with it, you argue, so . . . why not?

In some cases, this may indeed be the return to more co-operation and even a reconciliation. But I only see the cases which *don't* work. One partner or the other feels used, hurt, angry, feels 'sucked in', and then reacts by withdrawing to the opposite extreme, trying to see only the negatives in the ex-spouse. Soon the partner attacks – and the battle is on again.

I cannot honestly tell you to 'do it' or 'not do it'. Instead, my advice would be: 'Think before you act.' It might be quite helpful to just talk to the other partner about the tender feelings that have arisen, and about what may result from any sexual activity. You are certainly less likely to have problems if you are cautious.

CHAPTER 8

What If Your Ex- Isn't Co-operating?

All through this book, I have been urging you to co-operate with your ex-spouse in dealing with your children. I have dealt with the need to exchange information about the children, to develop and carry out joint strategies for handling problems, and even to get together as a couple in certain situations, such as consulting with school authorities.

It would be nice if this kind of co-operation were always easy to come by. But in real life it does not always work out that way. You may find your ex-spouse unco-operative, and to a degree that ranges from mildly annoying to seriously obstructionist to downright dangerous. In this chapter, I will identify some of the more frequently encountered problems, and try to suggest what you can do about them.

First, though, I must state one important qualification: I am *not* dealing with situations in which the ex-spouse is totally cut off from communication with you, or is so hostile that communication is virtually impossible; if your ex-spouse is thousands of miles away and is never in touch; if your ex-spouse has totally disowned you and the children; if your ex-spouse is institutionalised and seeks no contact (or is incapable of contact); if you have to lock your doors to protect yourself and your children physically from your ex-spouse; then your problems lie outside the scope of this chapter, and you require professional legal and possibly therapeutic help. For the purposes of this chapter, then, I am assuming that there *is* a custodial/access arrangement, that there *is* some continuing contact and dialogue between you and your unco-operative ex-spouse.

How do we classify unco-operative behaviour? How can we be sure it is really your ex-spouse's fault, and not your own emotions getting out of hand? What if your ex- is doing something that really is not all that bad for the children, but is bad for *you?* Do you keep quiet 'for the sake of the kids'? Do you strike back at every little thing? Is it normal to experience some conflicts? Or does 'co-operation' mean everything always has to be smooth sailing?

These questions are important, because it is often very difficult for a divorced couple to separate, in their own minds, the conflicts and issues that led to the divorce from the conflicts and issues that concern raising the children. For example, when a mother berates the visiting father for bringing the kids home past their usual bedtime, is her objection based *solely* on her assessment of what is best for the children? Or is she allowing some of the anxieties and hostilities that are still left over from her marriage to spill over into her role as a parent? Or maybe a little bit of both? And how do we evaluate her reaction if he brings them home two hours late? One hour late? Ten minutes late?

You should not feel upset or guilty if you can't always keep your two identities absolutely separate: your identity as ex-spouse, continuing some form of contact with a person who has caused you to be so unhappy; and your identity as a parent, trying to co-operate with this very same person in raising your children. All you can do is to try to be as objective as possible in evaluating what you believe to be unco-operative behaviour. What counts is *the children's welfare.*

Although there are many different forms of unco-operative behaviour by one or both parents, essentially they fall into these main categories:

1. Things that may be annoying (or worse) to you, but which aren't necessarily bad for the children;
2. Things that may be annoying (or worse) to you, and which are *also* bad for the children;
3. Things that do not directly affect you, but which can range from mildly bad to absolutely dangerous for the children.

Let's look at some typical case histories.

1. *'Why wasn't he like this before?'* During his stormy marriage to Lois, Jack Wilson had rarely spent much time with the children. Raising the kids was considered to be 'her depart-

ment'. As a busy, successful executive, Jack considered his
responsibilities fulfilled when he wrote the cheques. . . . But
after the divorce, Jack had an instantaneous transformation
and became Super-Dad. He was a genuinely and sincerely
devoted father. He put a lot of thought and effort into making
each visit as satisfying as possible. He phoned almost every
day. He demanded to see the children in between regularly
arranged visits. He checked up on every move that Lois made,
often questioning her judgements and decisions. (His questions
were always thoughtful and often valid too.)

Lois felt insecure, and eventually grew hostile. 'Why wasn't
he involved like this before?' she complained. Lois felt hard
done by; she had done all the work for all those years, and she
resented this sudden intrusion, even if it was difficult for her to
argue that Jack was not being a good father. After all, that was
the whole problem: he *was* being a good father. *Too* good,
maybe!

The Wilsons' story is one that I encounter very frequently
in my practice. It is difficult for a mother with custody to see
her ex- suddenly display a level of parental concern that was
not present before, to watch him getting the 'gravy' after she
has done all the work during those hard and thankless years
when he was unavailable.

But remember, we must look at what is best for the *children*.
If this increased involvement by your ex-spouse is beneficial to
them, you must not only allow it to happen, but encourage it.
If you fear that this new and better relationship between your
children and your ex-spouse will somehow make you look bad,
relax. It will not. The only way you lose is by fighting the new
reality, allowing your resentment to thwart a situation that, if
you are honest with yourself, you probably always wanted.
Didn't you used to wish he'd be more involved as a father?
Fine. Then be happy that he is finally doing it. There is a plus
in it for you, too – it gives you the opportunity to relax a bit, it
relieves you of the pressures of having to be 'all things' to your
children. In fact, we really should not consider this as a form
of unco-operative behaviour at all – although unfortunately it
is often presented to me in that light.

2. '*They're never ready when I get there!*' Frank McDonald never seemed to be able to get the children ready for their weekends with their mother, Diane. Somehow, breakfast was not quite finished yet. Or the children were not quite dressed. Or Frank was on the phone and could not let the children go until his conversation was finished, because he had some important last-minute instructions for them. One time, they were not there at all – Frank had let them go to a neighbour's to play for a while, and 'hadn't realised what time it was'. Diane was understandably frustrated. She yelled at Frank a few times, but he still kept doing it.

This is another very common problem. It can take another form, too: the visiting parent becomes the unco-operative partner, and habitually brings the children back home late.

In both cases, what is happening is very simple. The parent is resentful of having to 'hand the children over' to the other parent, and therefore concocts this little game as a means of expressing that resentment. When the other parent reacts by arguing, the unco-operative behaviour only escalates.

If you find yourself in this kind of situation, my advice is: do your best to tolerate it. Swallow your feelings, and try to avoid argument. If it is obvious that you are not willing to create a conflict, the other parent may respond in a positive way, and the problem will gradually diminish, or cease altogether.

It might not be very hard to take this in your stride if the inconvenience is only minor, a matter of a few minutes. But if it really begins to mess up your schedule, you are certainly entitled to respond.

Start by being as reasonable as you can. Mention the problem to the other parent, and ask for greater co-operation. Take the attitude that the other parent may not have understood the degree of inconvenience you have been experiencing, and will be more than willing to be more co-operative now that the problem has been made clear. *Do not* become holier than thou: 'I co-operate, why can't you?' 'You never were dependable, anyway!' 'Look how you're hurting the kids!' Ask quietly, and without insinuation, if the day was hectic, or the traffic was bad, or even if the pick-up and delivery times could be changed very slightly, to help make things easier.

When situations such as these are handled calmly, I have always found that the provocative behaviour is more likely to subside. But it you respond with righteous indignation, or with threats of retaliation, then you will soon be into a free-for-all, and the issue may never be resolved.

3. *'Look how he's ruining the children!'* Cheryl Rosenberg would have agreed with me that the first case history – the suddenly doting parent – really is not a problem, as long as the new-found commitment to the children is genuine and sincere. She would also have agreed with me that the second case history – 'nuisance-level' non-co-operation – is not worth going to war about either. But when Phil started shamelessly bribing the children during every single visit, Cheryl was ready to fight back with every means at her disposal . . . including trying to change the access arrangement.

Here, at last, was a case where the children themselves were being hurt! Phil did everything he could do to spoil them rotten. He took them to films, stuffed them full of sweets and junk food, let them stay up late, did not insist that they did their homework, let them get away with murder. It was round-the-clock party-time from the moment he picked them up to the moment he brought them back, tired, 'sick from all those sweets', rude to Cheryl, resentful at having to come back home to her more strict rules and regulations. Phil did his best to feed their resentment too. Whenever Cheryl questioned what he was doing, he condemned her – right in front of the children. He said she was too strict, that she did not want the children to have any fun. When he left, he always managed to get in a parting shot, like 'Don't worry, kids, we'll have a great time next weekend!'

As a responsible parent, Cheryl was understandably worried that Phil's excesses would prove harmful to the children. She feared they might fall behind in their work at school, develop bad sleeping habits, get cavities from all the sweets, and develop a warped sense of values. She saw clearly that Phil was trying to buy their affection and, worse, that he might be succeeding. She sensed herself being pushed into the 'wicked witch' role, and she resented having to do all the unglamourous slogging with the kids all week long, while Phil just breezed in on the weekends for fun, fun, fun. Soon she was deep in discussion with her solicitor. There was no way she was going to let Phil continue this way. For the good of the children, he had to be stopped.

This is another very common situation, and if you are now in the same position, you probably find it easy to identify with Cheryl's feelings, wanting to 'get' the no-good so-and-so and stop him from ruining the children. You may acknowledge that your own feelings of resentment may have something to do with it, but in your own defence you can point out that even if you were being as cool and objective as possible, you would still feel it necessary to intervene – and forcefully – purely for the sake of the children. As Cheryl said to me: 'Forget my own feelings. Certainly I'm mad at the position he's putting me in. But let's say I didn't pay any attention to that. As a mother worried about my children's welfare, am I not right in saying that what he's doing is bad for them? He's harming them! And when I tell him about it, he pays no attention. He laughs at me. I have to stop him, and I'll go to any lengths!'

Cheryl is right in her evaluation of Phil's conduct. The children are being wooed in the wrong way, and there may indeed be some harmful side-effects. Phil's lack of response to Cheryl's concerns adds fuel to the fire, demonstrating to the children that the parents are not co-operating, and also encouraging them to play one parent off against the other. But Cheryl's determination to fight back is *not* the correct approach. It is a solution that is worse than the problem.

You and your ex-spouse are separated or divorced because, for many reasons, you could not continue to exist together as a unit. You fought – but this did not help, because nothing was resolved. Yet you felt just as bad when you tried to avoid fighting – giving in made you feel like the 'loser', and you were already feeling lost enough as it was.

Now you are apart, and you have the chance to renew your own life. But your ex-spouse is making things miserable for you, causing you to have legitimate worries about your children and, at the same time, aggravating some of the anxieties or insecurities you were suffering during the marriage. So you want to fight back. But that did not work when you were married. Why will it work now?

Fine, you say, I will *not* do the fighting myself. I will get a lawyer to do it for me. The solicitor can bring my ex-spouse to heel. The solicitor can make my ex-spouse co-operate. The solicitor can get the access arangements changed or taken away altogether.

Think again. The fight will be long and bitter. A judgement will be handed down. But who is going to enforce the judgement, make sure the rules are kept? Will that judgement really stand? When will it next be challenged? Your ex-spouse will have a solicitor too. Soon you will both be back in court again.

There is another danger too. As you move into this new battle, you will begin to feel that, in order to win, you have to interpret practically every single action your ex- takes in a way that will begin to measure all your own moves to make certain everything you do is capable of being interpreted as favourably as possible. The moment this begins to happen – and it *will* happen – you lose all naturalness and spontaneity in your dealings with the children. You become more interested in doing not what may be best for the children, but what will *look* best in the eyes of the court, so that you can be sure of 'winning'.

And who 'wins', anyway? Nobody. When it is all over, *everybody loses*. You, your ex-spouse, and the children themselves.

I used to believe that the only real winners were the lawyers – the 'hired guns' who received handsome fees. But I have changed my opinion in the past few years. Happily, I am finding that the ruthless lawyer who could not care less about the welfare of the parents and the children is the exception; the rule is the responsible lawyer who looks towards some sort of compromise resolution of the problem, as opposed to winning or losing through the verbal battle in the courtroom.

As I have pointed out in an earlier chapter, I have never seen a bitter court-room fight in which the antagonists were treated as adults. The fact that they have to give up their right to speak for themselves, that they need other people to represent them, that they have to convince a judge that *they* are 'right' and the other person is 'wrong' – all of this is in itself a classic *childhood situation.* Two siblings argue and bring the argument to the parent (judge). Each is trying to prove something, but the apparent cause of the dispute is soon forgotten because the real issue is: 'Please tell me I'm the favoured child.' How can two adults who subject themselves to such a procedure continue to function as parents?

The children – the prize being fought over – are most often devastated by this on-going, drawn-out struggle. They will be harmed much more by the battle than they were by the problem that led to it. The damage Phil Rosenberg will do to his children by 'spoiling' them will be insignificant compared to the damage Cheryl will do by letting her retaliation extend all the way to yet another court battle.

What I am appealing for, then, is a close self-scrutiny. A look at your own feelings and motives, coupled with a *realistic* assessment of the real damage being inflicted on the children by your ex-spouse, compared to the damage that an all-out battle would inflict. Keep in your mind the picture of your children at the end of that battle – emotionally battered, torn, their loyalties divided, their guilt played upon, their respect for their parents (and, possibly, for themselves) lost. After evaluating all this, if you can see that there is something to be said for putting up with the situation (and yes, it is terribly unfair on you) – *put up with it.*

This does not mean you have to be completely passive, however. There *are* things you can do, short of an all-out war.

Set the best example for your children that you can. Keep to your standards. Let them see that there is some thought and integrity behind your standards, that they are not just a meaningless list of 'rules and regulations'. Children are quick to spot hypocrisy – if you quickly abandon the standards you have been setting, and get drawn into a popularity contest with your ex-spouse, the children will lose respect for you.

Talk to your children about the problem. Explain to them what you feel you have to do, and why you believe it is for their benefit. Be willing to answer any questions, if that helps to make the reasons for your policies clearer to them – but do not

130 *Divorced Parenting*

get apologetic or defensive. State very clearly that you do not agree with what your ex-spouse is doing, but add that this disagreement does not mean that the other parent is a bad person.

Point out to your children that they *do* have a choice in following certain standards, and that you hope they *themselves* will come to do what is right and what is best for them.

Remember that there are many situations, other than visits with your ex-spouse, in which you have relatively little control over the people, values and standards of behaviour to which your children may be exposed. When they go off to school, out with other young people, or even down the street to play at the home of a friend, they come into contact with environments that are different from your own. You know that a certain child will lead your children astray; that someone will eventually teach them to swear, or to try smoking; that the nice lady down the street will always let them watch that cowboy show or eat that extra piece of cake. And you probably accept these things because you know that your children recognise your standards and will come through okay anyway. Try to adopt that frame of mind for this situation, too.

If the children are old enough and mature enough, in your judgement, to handle this kind of information, then come right out and explain your decision not to get into a fight with your ex-spouse on this issue. Tell them you do not think a fight will solve anything, that they have to deal with their own feelings and decide (with or without your offered help) whether or not to deal with the other parent by themselves.

Recognise that, in the end, the children will come to some conclusion as to which one was the 'right' or 'wrong' parent. Usually they will come down on the side of the more sensitive, sensible and understanding parent – not the one who bribed them, not the one who is the best 'fighter'. When you respect yourself (by not abandoning your standards to be drawn into a popularity contest) and when you respect your children (by sharing with them your feelings about this issue) they will end up respecting *you*.

The above steps should be helpful if you find yourself in a situation similar to the case history I described. But what happens if your ex-spouse is doing something that is extremely harmful to the children?

I am referring to gross neglect, physical abuse, sexual abuse, chronic drug or alcohol problems, etc. I have mentioned this kind of problem briefly in a previous chapter, so I will simply repeat the advice: once you know that the harmful conduct really is happening (and is not an unfounded rumour), you have both the right and the responsibility to keep your children from all contact with your ex-spouse. Since a great deal depends on the specifics of the case, any suggestions I might make would probably be too vague or too general to be very useful. So my advice is: seek professional help *immediately*. Talk to your solicitor, doctor, therapist, social worker. A trained professional will be able to advise you on the best step-by-step course of action.

Be sure that what you are reacting to is *a real threat to the children* and not some aspect of your ex-spouse's lifestyle that may be reprehensible but does not impair his or her ability to be an effective parent. I once witnessed a bitterly contested custody case, in which the father turned out to be bisexual. He suffered a great deal socially, and even lost his job as a result. But he was a warm, sensitive and considerate father, who was much better able to deal with his young son than was the controlled, rather harsh and rigid mother.

I have also seen cases in which the mother's sexual promiscuity was used as an argument against her fitness as a mother, where in fact she proved to be an excellent mother, sensitive to and sensible with her children. There are people who may be ruthless and even violent in competitive situations, yet who are gentle, understanding and supportive with their children; conversely, I have seen many people who appear to be gentle, retiring and co-operative, yet who prove to be harsh and bullying with their children. So remember: the test is, 'Are the children being harmed?' If there is a serious danger to the children, don't hesitate to act.

4. '*She's turning them against me!*' Bob Leroy thought he was handling the post-divorce period very well. He was scrupulous about honouring all the conditions: the support payments were always in on time, he did not abuse his visiting rights, he even managed to accompany Beverley to the children's school for a chat with the principal. His personal life was better too: after being down in the dumps for the first couple of months, he was pulling himself together, doing well in his job, and was now involved in a relationship with a warm and understanding woman.

Gradually, however, a new problem began to surface. The children were displaying occasional bursts of hostility towards him. They said they had heard bad things about the woman he was going out with. They asked him why he had not been willing to pay for a school outing, which meant they could not go. It did not take long for Bob to work out where these bad feelings were coming from. It was Beverley. She was obviously putting ideas into their heads, twisting certain things and outright lying about others. (He had offered to pay for the school trip, for instance, but it was Beverley who said she did not want the kids to go – and, after some discussion, Bob had reluctantly agreed.)

An ex-spouse who attempts to turn your children against you is a particularly vexing – and all too frequent – problem. You will feel hurt and angry. You may even begin to resent your children for being parties to such a terrible injustice. What can you do about it?

If you opt to fight fire with fire, you will soon find yourself in a mud-slinging situation that will only intensify the struggle – and increase the children's problems. If you start to deny the allegations, and perhaps come back with a few of your own, you may temporarily feel better, but the children are almost certain to feel worse. Retaliation does two harmful things to your children.

It makes them feel both frightened and powerless in the face of this aggression between two parents whom they love, want to admire, and want to be close to. How can they admire people locked in mutual accusations? They cannot – and hence the fear (and possibly guilt, if the children believe that it is their talebearing that has caused the problem) arises. How can they stop the attack and counter-attack? They cannot – and hence the feeling of powerlessness, which reminds them of how they felt when you first told them of the divorce, returns.

It also places them in a role reversal situation. When you angrily deny accusations, or come back with some of your own, what you are really doing is telling the children that they are not your children but rather, your parents. They have to sit there, weigh the evidence, and determine which of the two adults is 'better' – in effect, which 'adult' is the better 'child' in the eyes of the 'parent', who is in fact the child! Are you confused by all this? Imagine how your children feel!

What do you do, then, if you are faced with this problem? You can show that you are puzzled by the other parent's allegations. You can express your concern about the other parent's attitude. Tell your children that you understand how this must make things difficult for them. Explain to them that at times, when someone is angry or hurt, they say things about other people that they would not normally say. Compare this to the times when the children themselves fight with each other, and say things to each other and about each other that they do not really mean to say. Tell the children that in time, you hope the other parent will stop doing this. If the children tell you how hurt they are, or that they don't like to hear these things about you, suggest they tell this to the other parent.

Your response, then, should be calm and reasonable. You are expressing your concerns honestly, without having to resort to counter-attack. You are showing your children that you identify with *their* problem and *their* feelings, instead of just rushing off into a flurry of self-justification that leaves them even more hurt and confused. This positive kind of response, one which addresses itself to the children's feelings and needs without undermining your own, is the response most likely to work in this situation.

5. *'You call these "visits"?'* The case histories I have presented so far all have to do with negative or unco-operative *actions*. But Heather Morton faced a different kind of problem: non-action.

Jerry had visiting rights, but rarely did he visit! Many times the children waited at the door, in eager anticipation, only for Jerry to show up an hour late, looking as if he wanted to be anywhere else in the world but there at that moment. Sometimes, he did not even show up at all. The visits themselves, when he did go through with them, were half-hearted affairs, and the children often came home as much as two or three hours ahead of the arranged time. All of this was very strange to Heather, because although their marriage had been a disaster, she never would have accused Jerry of being a disinterested father. He had always loved the kids, and they loved him. Why this strange behaviour all of a sudden? Could he not see what it was doing to the children? Did he *want* to hurt the children like this?

Yes, he did see what it was doing to the children. And no, he did not want to hurt them. I have seen this kind of situation occur many times, but rarely have I seen a parent do it out of a wish to hurt the children. What is going on, instead, is a strong feeling of uselessness as a parent, a feeling of being unwanted, un-needed. The parent then reacts by being irresponsible or insenstitive.

Blaming, nagging and accusing *will not help*. If you are the custodial parent in such a situation, start by telling the visiting parent, very calmly and factually, that the children are very disappointed when the arrangements are not kept. Suggest, gently, that perhaps the schedule is a problem. Is there any way you can help? Should it be changed?

Confidence-boosting is needed. Emphasise that both you and the children strongly believe that your ex-spouse is very valuable and important to the children as a parent, even though the two of you are no longer husband and wife. Does your ex- share your belief? If not, how can that negative feeling be changed? Be supportive – offer to help.

When you talk about how disappointed the children are at the aborted or haphazard visits, do not turn this into an accusation of neglect. Instead, treat it as an indication of how important this parent is in the children's lives.

If none of this helps, ask your ex-spouse if a hiatus in the visiting is appropriate. At the same time, voice your fear that this may lead to further alienation from the children, something which 'we all may eventually regret'.

The more you deal with this as a problem that you all share – rather than setting up your ex-spouse as a culprit who is being 'bad' – the better your chances of solving or alleviating the problem. If you are still not getting anywhere, you may eventually have to face up to the fact that you will have to deal with the children on your own, without the benefit of the other parent. Time – and your ability to deal sensitively with your children – will take care of the situation.

The children, of course, will feel sad and rejected. Do not use this as an excuse to put down the other parent. Do not blame your ex-spouse for being neglectful, rejecting, non-caring. Do not try to cover up for your ex- either, though. Instead, recognise that your children are experiencing the feelings of loss and guilt that we discussed earlier in the chapter on separating. They have lost, or are losing, one of their parents. What have they done to cause this awful situation? What can they do to get this parent back? Will *you* also leave them? What will they do with the feelings that overwhelm them? These are some of the questions and emotions at play here.

Tell them that you recognise how terrible they feel. Stress that they are not at fault. It is nothing that they have done, or not done. Explain that sometimes grown-ups cannot help themselves, and end up doing things that hurt their children, even though they do not mean to. You are sure that their other parent is not happy about what has happened.

Tell them you understand that they feel sad, maybe mad, maybe even scared about all this. But you are there now, and will always be there, to help them talk about it. Maybe talking about it will help them feel better. Allow them to express their feelings, be ready for resultant misbehaviour, and understand it, out loud, as being caused by these feelings. But ask them: is there a better way to handle these feelings?

Do not immediately jump into giving them a 'good time', out of the well-meaning but mistaken belief that this will help them forget. They must deal with their feelings. Do not force or encourage your children to mask them. By encouraging the feelings and helping your children to deal with them, you will be helping them to adjust to one of life's most difficult ideas: that of not being wanted, not being valued by someone you value. In time, they will start to value themselves again – and in that light they will re-evaluate their 'lost' parent in a more objective fashion.

CHAPTER 9

When Your Children Aren't Co-operating

If your children were fine prior to your separation and divorce, and if you handle the situation sensitively, then you can expect some short-term forms of protest, after which your children should adapt and do quite well. Some children even find the experience enriching.

There may be some temporary disruptions of emotional development, depending on the age of the children and the stage of development already reached. I dealt with the more common forms of regressive behaviour in an earlier chapter, but it may be useful to review them again quickly.

- *The one-year-old* will not understand what is happening, and will react to the reactions of the parents, sensing their feelings of anger, depression, guilt. This is particularly true of the child's relationship to the parent with custody. If that parent is the one who has been in charge of the child's care most, and if that parent recovers reasonably quickly, the disruption to the child should be minimal. The most common disturbances at this age include disruptions in eating habits (either loss of appetite or nervous overeating), sleep disturbances, nightmares, colic or other bowel disturbances, rashes or mild respiratory disorders.
- *The child who has just been toilet trained* may suddenly revert to wetting the bed, soiling his pants, spilling and breaking things. He may refuse to be left alone for any length of time, may start to cling, may have difficulty allowing the custodial parent out of his sight. He may also stop walking, and turn to crawling.
- *The three-to-four-year-old* may have to stick so closely to the custodial parent that he may have trouble playing with

others. He may refuse to attend nursery school. There may
be psychosomatic complaints, ranging from a sore tummy
to a sore throat, foot, or any other organ. The child may be
prone to colds and infections.

- *The child who has just learned to read* or do basic arithmetic
  may lose his excitement about his new skill. He may seem
  to lose all curiosity in the outside world, may retreat more
  into himself, nursing the hurt he has suffered. He may run
  away from the problem altogether, thus becoming harder
  to control, more likely to challenge and test parental
  authority. He may concentrate on friendships too much in
  order to avoid his home life and his own hurt feelings. In
  school, this child's difficulty with learning is a way of
  saying: 'Why should I find out new things? Look at how
  badly I feel about what I have already found out!' In a
  sense, all regressive behaviour is a way for the child to say,
  'Why should I hang on to this accomplishment, if instead of
  making myself and my parents happy, I've ended up hurt?'
- *The adolescent* often reacts with disdain, accusing his parents
  of lack of stability, lack of morality, lack of courage. He
  may blame them for not having separated sooner.
  Conversely, he may blame them for not caring enough
  about the children to stay together in spite of their marital
  problem. His willingness to pass judgement may make him
  very empathetic toward the parent he considers to be 'in
  the right'. He may try to replace the parent who has left the
  home, assuming a more 'adult' role towards the other
  parent. He is often quite helpful with younger brothers and
  sisters.

These, then, are the major kinds of temporary reactions to be
expected among children of divorced parents. The techniques I
have set out in earlier chapters should help you deal with these
situations. If the children previously have been behaving normally, and if you handle them as people, not as chattels to be
fought over, the problems should disappear, and the children
survive and adjust quite well.

But, of course, there are children who do not seem to be
responding or adjusting, who do not seem to be 'co-operating'

with all the neat 'do's' and 'don'ts' which I have set out in previous chapters.

The 'unco-operative' child should be seen as a child who is sending you a message. The message is: 'You are mistreating me. Or if you're not, then this whole situation is harming me.'

This child is not able to protest verbally and directly. (Remember that behaviour disruptions are really a form of protest, which diminish when feelings of love and security are re-established.) Or perhaps the child has already attempted a direct protest, through words or actions, but without much success. The child comes to the conclusion, 'What's the use?' And this triggers a new round of negative behaviour, which can be much more serious and deep-seated.

Let's look at some common examples.

The Manipulative Child

This child was hoping for a certain 'decision', or verdict, to emerge from the fight between his parents: a reconciliation, a resolution that the parents would stay together. It obviously did not work out that way.

But now he has made a new discovery: his parents are really fighting over *him*. He senses their guilt, and also understands that winning his favour is more important to the parents than he himself is. They care less about *his* happiness than about his approval of *them* (that is, their own happiness, their own 'victory' in the contest).

The child quickly concludes that he has to look after himself, and that he can play one parent against the other for the purposes of re-establishing his own self-esteem. It also gives him a sense of control over the situation that partially compensates for his previous feelings of powerlessness at not having been able to prevent the divorce. So the manipulation begins.

'Daddy, I'm so upset. Mummy wouldn't let me have those new trainers! I cried all night long. Oh, really? You'll buy them for me? Thank you, Daddy, thank you. You're super.'

'Mummy, Daddy didn't like you making me wear those plain brown shoes. I told him they were awful, and he agreed. He says you're really mean, and you don't care about me. By the way, you know that Johnny just got a super new pair of skates? I wish I could have a pair like that. Really, Mummy? Thanks, Mummy.'

The same technique works with bedtime, watching TV, not having to do homework, or making a point of describing one parent's 'new friend' to the other parent. The child does not even have to lie, just omit certain bits of information, present others out of context, and let his voice rise or drop for dramatic effect.

This child is not a bad child. He is just working the system that *both of you have set up*, and working it to his advantage.

DON'Ts

1. DON'T go along with it. Don't get into the bidding war for favours. Don't accuse the other parent of bribing, or having more money, or not allowing you enough money to be able to buy favours, too. Don't play on the child's sympathy, by telling him you cannot compete in the bidding war because you are too overworked, poor, tired, or underpaid.
2. DON'T show great curiosity for information about the other parent, eagerly awaiting each tit-bit that the child may deign to pass along.
3. DON'T ask the child to keep secrets. In particular, don't threaten the child that he had better not tell the other parent – or else.

DOs

1. DO stand firm. Despite possible protests and even accusations, your child will respect you for taking a strong position.
2. DO explain to the child that you feel you can provide him with understanding, which is what he really needs. Because of this, you have to do what *you* think and believe is right . . . which is why you will not always go along with his demands. DO tell him that you understand he may feel angry with you right now, but that in time you hope he will understand.
3. DO remain consistent, but also reasonable. Dropping out of

the bidding does *not* mean you totally cease to provide treats for your child from time to time. Your pattern should be to do what is natural, reasonable, understandable.

4. DO point out the harmful effects of this bidding war to the other parent. Ask if you have been doing something that has pushed your ex- into this war. Request the parent's support in ending it.

5. DO realise that the other parent may not be deliberately trying to undermine you and your position. The child may be quite a skilful manipulator, and you should not assume that the other parent is automatically at fault. The important thing to do is to set up communication between the two of you in order to stop the manipulative behaviour. This kind of behaviour is certainly not unknown in the happiest of families, and it always takes joint parental action to deal with it.

6. DO act quickly. This kind of problem must be nipped in the bud, or you will all be in trouble! If the other parent refuses to act along with you, then you drop out of the contest. In the long run, and in most cases I have followed, you and your children will *not* be the losers.

The Undisciplined Child

This child suddenly becomes resistant to any direction on your part. He just *will not* be disciplined. He is totally unco-operative. He fights with brothers, sisters, friends, classmates. The teachers at school tell you he is impossible to control.

Understand that this child is *not*

a becoming a monster;
b becoming just like your ex-spouse;
c out to punish you.

What he is doing is telling you that the emotional load has become too hard to handle. So the socially unacceptable behaviour that is normally controlled (in the sense that minor discipline problems are to be expected as a healthy and normal part of growing up) is now raging out of control. Another message that this behaviour can represent, is the plaintive, 'What's the use?' The child is asking, 'Why be good and follow the rules when you get hurt anyway?'

This kind of problem is usually most severe in families that have not encouraged the child to express his feelings. Yet feelings must be expressed, so if they are forcibly bottled up and cannot be voiced, they escape in some other way.

DON'Ts

1. DON'T accuse the child of being bad.
2. DON'T try to make him feel guilty for his misbehaviour by relating it to your own problems. Often the custodial parent will say, 'How can you do this to me when I've been left alone here and have so many other things to cope with?' Or the outside parent will say, 'How can you do this to me when I only see you once a week? Look – you're spoiling it for me!'
3. DON'T tell the child that he must be behaving better when he is with the other parent: 'I'll bet you don't act like this when you're with your Dad.'
4. DON'T accuse the other parent of spoiling the child, or setting the child up to misbehave with you.
5. DON'T ask the child what you can do with him, or buy for him, to persuade him to improve his behaviour.
6. DON'T become so overwhelmed by the child's change in behaviour that you start to blame yourself and feel guilty towards the child. This might cause you to go out and buy something for the child – a treat intended to reduce the child's anger towards you and to ease your own guilt.
Such a response would be inneffective and very inappropriate.

DOs

1. DO sit down with your child and, as calmly yet as forcefully as possible, explain what you think is happening, and why. Your argument should go like this: the child's new behaviour has come on since the recent change in lifestyle (separation or divorce); this new behaviour is not like him, and must therefore be due to some confused, disturbing feelings going on inside him; you know that he is uncomfortable because of these feelings and because he cannot talk about them and deal with them in a more constructive way; you do not like this new behaviour pattern and you are sure that he does not really like it either; you want to do something to stop this, and you are sure he does too; you are sitting down with him now, and you will continue to sit down with him whenever necessary, and whenever he wishes to talk about his unhappiness and anger. You will try to help him deal with it: you will not be able to get together with the other parent to mend the marriage, but you *will* sit down with the child to help him deal with his bad feelings about the divorce. As you have always done with the child in the past, you will continue – in spite of the fact that you understand its cause – to punish him for misbehaviour. Your punishments will not be unusually harsh, and they will not affect your willingness to talk with the child about his feelings, and to help him express those feelings. You are sympathetic, but you will also be firm in disciplining the child for misbehaviour.

This discussion accomplishes some important things. It lets the child know that *you* know how he is feeling, and that you are available to help him develop better ways of expressing these feelings. At the same time, by stating your unhappiness with his behaviour and your determination to punish misbehaviour, you are showing the child that you have not relinquished the parental role. Although on the surface he may display some hostility towards your punishments, deep down he will begin to feel more secure in the knowledge that, despite the divorce, you are continuing to be an effective parent.

2. DO call the other parent to discuss what has been happening. Ask if this kind of behaviour happens with that parent as well. Do not accuse the other parent of contributing to the problem, but ask for help in dealing with a problem that you *both* share. Explain how you have handled the situation thus far – your discussion with the child as outlined above – and ask for help, advice, and co-operation.

3. DO be on the lookout for a spill-over of undisciplined behaviour on to the other children in the family. Your children may all fight more than usual. Such fighting is not only an expression of internal turmoil, but also a message that they doubt your ability to keep the family together. Sit them down and talk to them as a group. Point out that you are both willing and able to look after all of them. Explain that this is a difficult period for all of you, but that you are counting on each of them to do his share, and you will do yours.

The Secretive Child

This child has not yet shared the details of the divorce with his friends or teachers. He shows signs of being afraid to go to school, to go out with friends, or to have friends stay the night at the house. He may also show a reluctance to return home to the custodial parent after a visit, or else be reluctant to leave the custodial parent when the visiting parent arrives. You must handle this situation in a similar way to any other difficulty the child has. His phobia, whatever its nature and intensity, is simply one more way of dealing with the traumatic feelings he has regarding the divorce. An additional factor that is so often at work with this child is his feeling that somehow his unhappy situation is unique, and shameful. He is afraid of being isolated, teased, or ostracised by friends or teachers for being part of a family that has been struck by divorce.

Explain to the child that his problem is not unique, that there are many children in the same situation, and that you are certain that if he tells his friends what has happened, they will be understanding and sympathetic. Point out to the child that his behaviour will isolate him far more than the divorce itself will. This behaviour will invite hostility from friends who will *not* understand its cause.

If the child needs it, offer to accompany him to speak to teachers about this. When you get there, do not abandon the child – make sure your discussion with the teachers takes place in the presence of the child. As far as informing his friends is concerned, it is probably better if the child does this himself, without your being present. But by all means offer to help him rehearse what he is going to say.

Keep stressing that the divorce is not the fault of the child. Yes, he may feel badly about it, but that does not mean he himself is a bad person, or foolish, or stupid.

In spite of your reassurances, your child may come across the occasional insensitive playmate who may use the news as a weapon. Handle this the way you would any teasing about any other issue: in other words, it is the same as if your child were being teased for being short, or fat, or a 'bookworm'. The teasing does not have some unique quality merely because it happens to be around the issue of divorce.

Point out to your child that other people have fears and anxieties that cause them to tease. Also, encourage your child to take such behaviour in his stride without giving in to self-pity. Point out all the other friends, teachers and relatives who have not teased but who have been very supportive. Your own love for the child, plus any sense of self-confidence that you are able to convey, should be very helpful.

The child who is afraid to go to the visiting parent, or to return to the custodial parent, is usually reacting to one of two things:

a The parent may be doing something that is frightening to the child, and the child feels like an accessory to a crime. The parent may have a 'new friend'; parent and child may be doing activities together of which the other parent may not approve; the parent may be asking the child to keep something secret.

b The parent may be showing great reluctance to let the child spend time with the other parent, and the child somehow feels he must ally himself with the 'hurting' parent.

In either case, review your behaviour and check with your ex-spouse on what may be happening to cause the child's reaction. *Solve it quickly.* Make certain that you are not using the child, or brainwashing him, or in any other way putting him in the position of having to 'protect' you, or 'inform' to you, or somehow do your work in an unfortunate duel with your ex-spouse. If you and your ex-spouse can work it out quickly, the child will *not* be unco-operative.

The three examples I have given – the manipulative child, the undisciplined child, and the secretive child – are the most typical illustrations of how a child can be unco-operative. In all three cases, the child's behaviour becomes just another way of expressing the feelings of anxiety caused by the divorce. In all three cases, it is important to let the child know that you understand his feelings, and to encourage him to express those feelings in a more positive, or less destructive, way.

In spite of the steps I have recommended, you may still find the child's behaviour continuing. If that happens, then you should consult your family doctor, solicitor, or friends who have been through similar struggles, to find a professional person (such as a psychologist, psychiatrist or social worker) to help all of you deal with this issue.

Re-marriage

If, like many divorced people, you decide to get married
again, you can expect to encounter certain problems with your
children. In the majority of cases, none of these problems will
be brand new, or come as a complete surprise. Most, if not all
of them, will have already been brewing. The reason is simple.
You are probably getting married to a person with whom you
have already had some kind of lengthy relationship. That relationship had to be explained to your children in the first place,
and that was where the problems first surfaced. Your decision
to formalise that relationship through marriage simply means
those problems will continue for a while. But it does not
necessarily create any new problems. So my first piece of
advice is: re-read the chapter on 'Your New Life', dealing with
the problems you face when informing your children of a
new relationship, and helping them adjust to it. That
information should help you with this next step.

But while the problems themselves may not be different, I
recognise that there certainly is a different quality to them now.
It is one thing to introduce a 'new friend'. It is quite another to
present the children with your new spouse!

The scope of the problems you will face depends on several
factors. For example, a lot will depend on how soon after your
divorce this new marriage takes place. If a relatively short
period of time has elapsed between divorce and re-marriage,
you can expect a fairly vigorous protest from the children. You
should recognise that this protest has less to do with the new
marriage than with the children's continuing need to resolve
their feelings and frustrations about the divorce itself. It is as if
you have moved on to Step Two, while they are still struggling
with Step One.

The split-up of their family is still a recent event and they
are still grappling with it. They are getting used to the pattern

of visits from the parent without custody. They may be suffering through some regressive behaviour. They may be adjusting (or afraid of adjusting) to school, friends, family. Now along comes another change, another adjustment, a 'new father' or 'new mother' – a step-parent. It all adds up to another reason for them to feel anxious or insecure. So their protest, when it comes, is more an expression of this insecurity, this emotional turmoil, than it is a rational judgement on the 'wisdom' of the the step you are taking, or the suitability of your new spouse. Yet their language, and the issues they express, may centre on these topics.

Another factor is the sex of each child. Children of the opposite sex to you, particularly if a lot of time has elapsed since the divorce, may have moved right into a position of feeling and acting (either in reality or in fantasy) as if they were your ex-spouse. Now you have a new adult to actually *be* your spouse, thus 'replacing' the child. The child, understandably, is reluctant to give up that privileged position. So your remarriage must be opposed.

A third factor is the parental status of your new mate. Your own children may resent any attention you give to your friend's children. They will see it as something that is being stolen from them, a way in which they are 'losing' you, just as they have already lost their other parent.

A fourth factor is ... you. You can be under a tremendous amount of emotional stress now. On the one hand, you are working hard on a new relationship. You may be experiencing the first feelings of romance and excitement that you have had in years. On the other hand, you are doing this at a time when your children's needs have increased. You will feel divided. You may even feel resentful towards your children, seeing their demands as something that robs you of the euphoria that is rightfully yours. Yet it is critically important to work with the children early and intensively, because the situation has the potential for great success or great failure.

DOs

1. Introduce your new friend as soon as you feel the relation-

ship is quite serious. This will be particularly meaningful to your children if you have not previously introduced each and every new companion. The children will know you are more than just casually interested in this new person.

2. Introduce the friend *in stages*. Don't foist this new person's presence on the children for any long intensive period too early. Take it gradually – the introduction, the new friend being 'around' for a while and then leaving you alone with the children, and, finally, all of you going on outings together.

3. Ask your children how they feel about this person. Let them know that their feelings, likes, dislikes are important to you. On the other hand, make sure they know that you intend to see other people and would like, eventually, a permanent relationship. You have your interests and needs, too. The children do not have *veto* power.

4. Be as frank as possible in answering their questions about whether you might marry this person. Keep them informed about the possibility of such a decision.

5. Let your ex-spouse know about your intentions. This will allow your ex- enough time to handle the feelings this news causes, and to handle them alone, or together with you. This honesty on your part should help gain your ex-spouse's support in dealing with the children.

6. Be prepared for a negative reaction from your ex-. Here, we are concerned about how the parental role complicates the reaction. Your ex-spouse, particularly if *you* have custody, may feel threatened by your new marriage, fearful that it will somehow mean this parent's displacement from the children's life. This can lead your ex-spouse to (consciously or unconsciously) set up conflicts between the children and you. If you can reassure your ex- that you do not intend to substitute your new spouse as the children's other parent, you have a much better chance of enlisting your ex-'s help in dealing with your children.

7. Ask your ex-spouse to talk to *you*, and not to the children, about any problems regarding your new marriage.

8. If at all possible, introduce your ex-spouse to your new partner, in order to discuss the children. If the two of them

can be allies where the children are concerned, it will be
extremely helpful.

DON'Ts

1. DON'T spring the new relationship on the children
suddenly.
2. DON'T try to force the 'chemistry' between your children
and your new partner. This will take time. Allow it to happen
gradually.
3. DON'T deny that you are seriously involved with the new
friend, and that you may get married. Such denials may
temporarily pacify the children, but will only cause more
serious problems later on.
4 DON'T deny or ignore your children's protests. Listen to
them, and try to deal with them as sensitively as possible.
5. DON'T let your children be the ones to tell your ex- about
the new relationship, thus forcing them to be the bearers of
'bad news'. Apart from putting unfair pressure on the
children, this also deprives your ex-spouse of the time needed
to deal with the news (and, possibly, discuss it with you)
before seeing the children. Your children will then be exposed
to your ex-spouse's *immediate* reaction. This may create a
conflict in their minds regarding where to place their loyalties.
Their exposure to your ex-spouse's spontaneous reaction
(particularly if that reaction is a combination of anger, fear,
guilt, resentment) may encourage them, in turn, to react
negatively towards your new companion, as they blame this
person for having caused such pain to their parent.

I realise that it sometimes may not be possible to follow this
advice. You may, for example, be at the early stages of a
relationship and not yet certain that it will end in re-marriage.
You feel strongly enough to want to introduce this new friend to
the children, but it is far too early to talk of marriage, either
to the children or to your ex-spouse. So you present the new
friend to the children in a fairly casual way, following my
recommendation about doing things in stages. But, surprise!
Your children immediately jump to conclusions and present

those conclusions to your ex-spouse at the next available opportunity.

There is no foolproof way to guarantee that this will not happen! All you can do is try to let your ex-spouse know about your intentions as soon as you yourself are sure of them. But if, as hard as you try, the children still pre-empt you, you will just have to explain to your ex-spouse, as honestly and as sympathetically as you can, that the children were being premature, that you had not said anything yet because you still had not decided, and that you certainly will not keep it secret once a decision is made. If your communication with your ex- has been open and co-operative on other issues – and we have touched on many of them in the previous chapters – then you should be able to work around this problem without any great difficulty.

Post Re-marriage Changes

The steps I have recommended above should help you deal with your children's reactions and adjustments to the news of your re-marriage. But there will be further adjustments after the marriage itself takes place.

After all, there may be many important changes in your life, and in the children's life. There may be a move to a new home. Or your new partner (with children?) may move into your present home. There may be a move to a new city. There may be marked changes in income or in lifestyle. All of this has to be worked through slowly, carefully, and sensitively.

First and foremost, do not try to 'sell' any of these changes. Always allow the children to voice their doubts and fears, and deal with each child separately, as an individual. Each of your children is at a different stage of development, and each will have a different set of questions, fears, hopes and wishes.

Some of the questions about physical or logistical changes have been covered earlier in this book, in the chapter on 'Separating'. Re-read the sections that focused on a new home, new town, new school or neighbourhood. Remember to let the child express his anxieties – do not try to squelch these fears under a barrage of jovial reassurances that there is nothing about which to worry. Once the fears are out on the table, you can look at them sensitively, using some of the techniques I have already presented.

There will be some issues, not covered in previous chapters, that derive from your new status as a *spouse* once again, and from the children's being forced into a relationship with a new adult and, possibly, new siblings. Some of the major issues are:

Your sex life The children may want to know about your sexual activity with your new partner. You should answer as directly as possible, but first assess *the reasons why* your child is asking. I have seen children worrying about this from points of view ranging from the morality of your action, to jealousy, to fear for your safety (the idea that you are somehow being *forced* into sexual activity), to guilt or jealousy caused by the experience of their own sexual feelings towards your new spouse. When I say you should answer 'directly', I do not mean that you should give explicit information. You can simply say that you have needs and desires, and you are looking after them. What you should *not* do is skirt the issue and refuse to discuss the topic at all. You should really handle this no differently than if the children were asking parents who are not divorced about their sexual activity.

Adoption Occasionally, when your children's other parent is completely out of the picture, your new spouse may legally adopt your children. It is relatively unusual for a court to sanction such a step-parent adoption. This is a very sensitive issue, and it must be very carefully discussed and worked through. It must not be forced upon the children. The children may have quite strong feelings either for or against this, especially if it involves a change of surname. The court will appoint a social worker to help you, and the children's feelings must be taken into account before a final decision can be made.

Change in your surname If you are a woman, you may decide to take your new husband's surname, which will be different from the one being used by your children. Your children may have great difficulty explaining this to their friends. They may certainly want your advice on how to handle it. Be alert to this situation, and ready to deal with it. Remember earlier techniques I discussed. First, ask the children for their ideas about resolving the problem; then suggest your own. Search for a compromise, if it is needed.

What to call your new spouse Deal with this in the same way as the issue of your new surname. Explain to your children: that they are not to feel pressured into calling your new partner Mum or Dad just to please the adults; that you are aware that they may actually wish to call the new spouse Mum or Dad but that they also feel the division of loyalty, and feel that they are betraying their actual other parent. Suggest that they come up with a name that sounds like Mum or Dad, something of their own creation. Emphasise that their *relationship* with your new spouse is more telling than any name the children decide upon.

Your relationship with your new spouse With luck, you will have a loving and rewarding relationship with your new spouse. Your children may fear that this love will lessen your love for them. It will be important for you to be able to reassure them on this score. This means explaining that adult love is different from love of children, and that one does not exclude the other. Tell them that if they think they see signs that you are not paying enough attention to them, they should speak up and let you know straight away.

Their feelings towards your new spouse Your children may feel that you expect them to love your new spouse – soon to be their step-parent – and may be fearful of your reaction if they do not.

Explain that you do not necessarily expect them to love your new partner; all you expect is that they learn to co-operate and live with this person, in the same way your new mate will co-operate with them.

Their feelings on this issue may be complicated by the love they still feel towards your ex-spouse, who remains, after all, their parent. They may believe that if they even *like* your new spouse, they are somehow betraying their other parent. Conversely, they may worry that if they continue to love their other parent, they are somehow betraying you.

You must help them draw the distinction between your feelings and their feelings, in relation to both your new spouse and your ex-. Explain that you have the right to your own feelings, and they have the right to theirs – and the two sets of feelings can exist independently. One does not necessarily harm or detract from the other.

You can use examples from their own experience with brothers, sisters, and friends. A brother can love a sister, and when a new baby arrives they can both love the new baby without jeopardising their original love for each other. The same holds true with friends – they can have several friends at the same time, without one friendship detracting from another. The can love and respect a teacher without it undermining their love for you, or for their other parent. By showing them that several sets of feelings can exist at the same time – each valid, each unimpaired by the other – you will help them become more relaxed about their feelings.

Stress that you do *not* necessarily expect them to view your new partner as a new father or mother but as a step-parent. All you want is their respect for your new spouse's authority as an 'adult' within the home.

Attending your wedding If there is to be a formal wedding, it is very important for the children to attend, and to be as involved as possible. If your relationship with the ex-spouse allows this, it is usually comforting to the children to have your ex- attend the wedding, too. I realise that this may be a very idealistic recommendation, and may well be impossible in most cases. The point is this: if the children can feel that *all* the parties are 'endorsing' the marriage, it will help their adjustment considerably. If it is unrealistic to expect your ex-spouse to be there, at least let us hope that your ex- can comment favourably on the wedding, and be enthusiastic about the children's attendance.

Attendance at the children's school or out-of-school activities I hope that you and your ex-spouse have both been attending functions that are important to your children. Now there is a third person to think of. Does the step-parent attend too? Does your ex-spouse stop attending? Do all of you sit together? How do you work it out?

The ideal is for all three of you to attend. Where you sit is less important. It will probably be most comfortable to have you and your new spouse sitting together, and your ex-spouse somewhere else. But at least if all of you are there, your children will feel much better. It is much easier for them to explain to their friends a divorce followed by co-operation than it is to explain a divorce followed by squabbling and manipulation.

The ideal may not be achievable, however. Your ex-spouse and your new companion may not be able to tolerate each other, and you may be unwilling to be caught in the middle of an afternoon or evening full of unspoken tension. So instead of all three of you going, you will have to work out a system. Perhaps you can attend alternate functions, you and your new spouse going to one, and your ex- going to the other.

You may even have to advise your new partner not to attend any functions at all, that you will go and your ex-spouse will go. You have to present this as something that is necessary, for the good of the children. Assure your new partner that this does not mean you have suddenly fallen out of love, or that you are suddenly getting back together with your ex-, or that the children object to the partner's presence. Your new spouse will have to be understanding. Things will work out. (With luck, you will have chosen an understanding and patient new spouse. If instead you have picked an obstinate, stubbornly possessive one, then you may be heading for a troubled marriage one more time.)

Getting along with your new spouse's family What if your new spouse has children? This can be a very volatile area which, if ignored, can quickly become a major battleground and even lead to the breakdown of your new marriage.

If possible, even *before* the two sets of children meet each other, and preferably long before you re-marry, you and your new companion must have a long and detailed discussion. Review the ages and personalities of the children. What are their levels of emotional and physical maturity? What kinds of friends do they have? What are their interests? Their likes and dislikes? What problems did they have adjusting to your divorce – and your new spouse's divorce (assuming, of course, that your new spouse is not widowed).

Look carefully at each child's position in the 'original' family – and in the 'new' blended family. For example, your eight-year-old eldest daughter may be devastated at suddenly having to cope with a nine-year-old 'older sister', but may also be elated to suddenly have a six-year-old 'younger step-brother'

to teach and 'boss around'. She may be excited at having a
fourteen-year-old sister (less threatening than a nine-year-old)
to emulate. Another example: your four-year-old son may resent a new two-year-old 'sweetie-pie' who will take over his
position as the pet of the family. But he will love the idea of
suddenly having three older step-siblings to dote upon him.

There may be fireworks between two teenagers of the same
sex being forced on each other, especially if one is 'with it',
popular, athletic, etc., while the other one is more inhibited and
not so popular. On the other hand, they may complement each
other and make a great combination.

Another kind of fireworks is the sexual kind. Your fourteen-
year-old daughter and your new spouse's sixteen-year-old son
may get along *too* well – and not have to worry about it, either,
because they are not really brother and sister, though they are
step-siblings.

Another item on your checklist should be the custodial or
access arrangements for each set of children. There are many
combinations: both you and your new spouse may have custody; one of you may have custody, the other access rights; one
of you may be in a relationship with a co-operative ex-spouse,
the other may still be embroiled in a bitter fight which involves
very unpleasant, negative contact between the children and the
other parent.

Evaluate what changes will take place in the children's life-
styles. Who is moving into whose house? Who has to now share
a bedroom, desk, etc.? All of this has to be considered very
carefully, and examined closely, because there really is the
potential for a tremendous explosion. Remember that in situations involving two sets of children, you are *not* marrying your
new spouse alone: your children, and your new spouse's children, are very much in the picture, and the great love you and
your new spouse feel for each other can quickly disintegrate in a
deluge of children's fights, parental feelings of guilt, taking
sides, protecting your own children or going overboard to
protect your step-children. *The possibilities for problems are enormous.*

After you have had this discussion, you should be 'tuned in'
to the kinds of problems that may develop once the two sets

of children get together. Naturally, you will not be able to anticipate everything, and there may be both pleasant and unpleasant surprises. But at least both of you will be somewhat familiar with each other's children, if only in theory. The next step is to put the relationship into practice.

1. Talk to your own children about your partner's children. Describe them as honestly as possible, stressing the positives but avoiding extremes of judgement or editorialising.
2. Ask your children what they think. Let them react as freely as possible.
3. After you've 'introduced' your companion's children to your own children in this way, let your children hear your companion's description of the children.
4. After your children have heard both descriptions, it is a good idea to show them pictures of the new children.
5. Follow the same steps with your partner's children. Finally, bring the two sets of children together. Follow the same steps in introducing your children to those of your new spouse. Let your new spouse do the talking first, then you, then pictures, then the meeting.
6. Tell all the children that you hope that they will get along well together. At the same time, explain that you understand that there may be occasional conflicts, and that both you and your partner will be there to help the children understand them and work them out.
7. Bring them together gradually. Start with short outings together. Work up through longer outings, weekends together, vacations, and finally living together. Each time a get-together is over, review your own children's feelings about how things went. What did they like or dislike? What worries them? What are they eagerly anticipating? What are they afraid of? Be patient, and do not condemn any of their reactions.
8. Once you are all living together, hold regular family meetings. The children can talk about their feelings (some will have to be dealt with individually), and certain issues can be looked after. In particular, family meetings are a good way to resolve conflicting standards of discipline, household routines and other policies.

9. DON'T RUSH. DON'T PUSH. DON'T CAJOLE. DON'T BEG. DON'T THREATEN.

10. If you are running into problems that do not seem to be going away, even with time and patience, do not hesitate to consult the Step-Family Association or a specialist in family therapy.

Remember that for *all* aspects of your children's adjustment to your new marriage, the three key words are TIME, TALKING and PATIENCE.

CHAPTER 11

Beyond Survival: Enrichment

A divorce can be compared to any severe psychological stress. It can even be compared to a disabling physical injury. Initially, the trauma gives rise to a great deal of self-doubt. There has been a blow to your ego, to your self-esteem. And your response can take you in several different directions.

One is to surrender to this self-doubt, to wallow in self-pity. 'Nobody cares for me,' you say. 'It's a lousy world. I can't do anything about my problem. Poor me.' People who stay in this frame of mind for more than a very brief period may wind up as emotional cripples. They deny themselves – and their children – any chance for further maturation. They do not marry, they do not succeed in relationships, and some of them drift towards alcoholism, drug addiction and failure in careers. All of which serves to fulfil the initial self-pitying predictions. 'Why should I try anything? I'll only fail. The world owes me something, but since it's such a lousy world, there's no hope for me anyway.'

Another direction is to become cynical. 'I can't trust anyone except myself,' you argue. 'But I can go out and get what I want for myself. I'll step on anyone along the way. They don't care, so why should I?' So you learn how to use people for your own purposes, and discard them when you no longer need them. Your divorce has left you hardened and embittered.

This approach can lead to success in business, perhaps, but it certainly does nothing in the way of interpersonal development, and it exerts a deadly influence on your children. You all survive – but you all live half a life – cynical, empty of permanent personal relationships.

There is a third direction – the direction that starts with survival and culminates in *enrichment*. You do not just 'get by'. You grow and develop and lead a richer, fuller life.

But before I explore this third option, let's backtrack for a moment and take a look at how people survive other forms of trauma. Can we learn anything that would help us respond to the trauma of a divorce?

Dr Karl Menninger has written that many people can go through severe personal problems, even emotional break-downs. However, if they receive the proper care, gain insight, and develop hope and determination, they cannot only survive but can go on to do much better. I have seen it happen time and time again. Why does a Helen Keller become an example to the whole world, instead of being an anonymous patient in some chronic care institution? How does a Beethoven write a symphony while totally deaf? How did George Shearing or Stevie Wonder – both blind – or Michael Flanders, a polio victim, overcome their handicaps to become major talents?

We can compare emotional damage with physical damage. When an artery to the heart is blocked off, the person sometimes dies – but more often, with the proper care and nurturing, with time and, yes, with luck, auxiliary pathways open and the person can survive for a long time. The human body can survive enormous damage. If the heart disease has been controlled and is not chronic and continuous, proper care enables you to survive, and go on from there. *Even if something has been damaged, what is left is of value – and is usually enough with which to survive.* It is exactly the same with emotional damage.

The heroes who overcome physical handicaps – be they a Roger Bannister dazzling the world, or a housewife running her home from a wheelchair – have all realised that *even if something is damaged, what is left is of value.* That realisation could have come quickly or slowly, spontaneously or through therapy ... but one way or another, they have all had it, and it is the key to their survival and fulfilment. The people who remain bitter and frustrated, on the other hand, have *not* had this realisation. They see only the damage, and not what is left over.

So it is with emotional and psychological damage ... like a divorce. The people who give in to self-pity, or become bitter and cynical, see only the damage. They do not see what is left over: the abilites, qualities and relationships that they still have, and that these can provide the springboard to a happier and fuller life.

How can you achieve that fuller life? To start with, go back to our comparison of divorce and *physical* trauma; the first step is to deal extensively with the acute disease. The disease must not be allowed to settle in and become chronic. Damage has been done, but now we must limit that damage, contain it, and see that we suffer no additional damage.

That has been the main purpose of this book: to help you make sure that the struggles do not go on indefinitely; to show you how to limit the negative features of your divorce; to point out positive and constructive things you can do.

My recommendations should help you cure the illness and get on with the rehabilitation. How?

DOs

1. *Take your time*. Allow yourself the time, energy and effort it takes to work through the feelings of loss engendered by your divorce. Allow your children the time too.
2. Remember that this is a time for self-examination, not self-condemnation. The marital break-up may have been due to problems with both you and your ex-spouse. If you can review the marriage and come to an understanding of what went wrong, and why, you then have the chance to correct certain problems in your future relationships. You have the chance to learn and grow from this experience.

On the other hand, you may simply have been the victim of your ex-spouse's desire to break up the marriage. If that is the case, you must make sure not to over-react to your feelings of desertion, either by sinking into a despondency (acting like the loser you perceive yourself to be) or attempting to punish your ex- for leaving you. You could not have prevented the divorce by yourself. But now the rest *is* up to you ... and you alone. Try to see this as something positive: you *can* influence events, you *don't* have to be helpless and drifting, it *is* in your power to rebuild your life.

3. Use the time to do some of the things you could not do in your marriage. This is a perfect time to do some travelling, for example, if you can manage it without interfering with your children's lives. The same applies to pursuit of a career, further education, etc. This will be particularly important if you feel your previous marriage was hampered by your (real or imagined) deficiencies or limitations in some of these areas. Okay, you had those limitations. But that is water under the bridge. The damage has been done. Pay attention to what is left over ... the rest of your life. Now you can use that time to grow.

In your relationship with your children, you have to face the fact that your divorce – any divorce – is painful and traumatic for the children. If, however, you can stand by them and not give up parenting, instead involving yourself more closely with them, helping them deal with this severe pain, you can actually develop a relationship that is unique. People who have survived difficult times together seem to develop a special friendship and closeness. If you can do this with your children, then you will establish a pattern of co-operation and sensitivity. All of you will profit from this. Your relationship can then, potentially, be a much better one than it would have been had you glibly sailed along in your marriage believing that simply because you maintain a two-parent home, you are properly parenting your child.

And another potential area of growth lies before you. Although your marriage is over and you may hate, even detest, your ex-spouse, you may find that you can develop your emotional maturity to deal with that person without vindictiveness, retaliation, tit-for-tat or tug-of-war, and you can overcome these impulses to deal constructively, compassionately and effectively with your role as parent to your children.

DON'Ts

1. Don't let yourself listen to unrealistic criticism by your ex-spouse.
2. When you review 'what went wrong', don't use this as an

excuse to pound yourself into the pavement, into depression or self-pity. Don't become obsessive about the past.

3. Don't do the opposite, either, and run away from any self-examination or examination of your marriage and its break-up.

4. Don't rush into a serious romantic relationship simply to avoid the pressures of loneliness, depression and self-doubt. The relief will be temporary, and you will soon face an even worse barrage of problems.

If you take the time to review your past and present situations, if you can tolerate the self-examination, if you can push yourself to take the proper steps to improve your problems, then you will be growing and maturing. You will be teaching yourself what to look for and avoid in a future partner or, if you choose not to marry, what to do to fulfil yourself so that your future will be one of enrichment – not bereavement. And that personal enrichment has an added bonus: inevitably, you will be a better parent.

25 Questions
Parents Often Ask Me

Q: My wife and I are about to separate, and will be telling the children within the next month. They do not know anything about it yet. Or at least that is what I thought ... until I found my eleven-year-old crying in bed last night. He told me that he had had a nightmare in which his mother and I had divorced. I told him it must have been a terrible dream, and patted him on the head until he fell asleep. What do I do now?

A: Your son obviously knows more than you have given him credit for. I believe he was using the avenue of the 'nightmare' to open up with you a discussion of your impending separation. I am happy that you did not tell him there was nothing to worry about, which would have been an abuse of his trust. He has enough to handle now without being lied to. That you empathised with him about how badly he must feel, and that you stayed to comfort him without denying the validity of his feelings, is important. You will have to do a good deal of that, in helping him face his upcoming struggles.

However, it is clear that your son should be told about your decision soon. Talk it over with your wife and see if you can move forward the planned date of telling the children.

Q: I am ready to re-marry. I have a daughter, five years old, whom my fiancé adores. I would like to end my ex-husband's visits with her, so that my new husband and I can both act as her parents without complications.

A: If your daughter and your ex-husband had the normal parent–child contact, then by now they are likely to have a firm and very important relationship – especially important to your daughter. In spite of her behaviour towards and acceptance of your fiancé, I am certain that there is no doubt in her mind about her true father's identity.

There may, however, be considerable doubt in her mind about your reaction to her relationship with your new boyfriend, and with her own father. *Don't* make it an 'either-or' situation, and *do* allow her and encourage her to continue her relationship with her father. You can have a new life with your new boyfriend, but in your daughter's best interests she should be allowed the benefit of a lasting relationship that does not depend on your change in marital status.

Q: I have recently separated, and will be divorcing my husband. I have a new boyfriend whom I will marry as soon as the divorce is final. We have a daughter, five months old, who treats my new boyfriend as a father. I really would like to cut off all access to my former husband, so that I can give myself and my new husband-to-be a proper chance to parent this child together.

A: *If* you have in fact been the main caretaking parent in your infant's life, and *if* your new boyfriend will in fact be joining you in a permanent relationship, and *if* he also wishes to be the 'psychological father' of your daughter, then you are already really presenting yourselves to her as her parents. At this age, it would be quite likely that she is already identifying your new boyfriend as 'father'. Any relationship maintained by her biological father at this stage would therefore be for his benefit, rather than for the child's. Although this may seem unfair to him, remember we are dealing here with what is best for the child.

Q: When she left me and the children, my wife also cleaned out our bank account. My solicitor and my parents tell me that I am being a sucker by allowing her to visit the kids. They claim I should keep her out until she gives me back some of the money. The kids are four, eight and ten.

A: She has been their mother, continues to be their mother, and always will be their mother. This relationship has *nothing* to do with her cleaning out your bank account. You may certainly have to settle the bank account issue through your solicitor, and possibly through the courts, but refusing to allow her to see the children would only serve to hurt and confuse them – and the children have likely been hurt and confused enough by the separation. They do not need to be used as a bargaining tool to help you regain the contents of your bank account!

Q: My son Johnny, ten, is away at a holiday camp for the first time. There is only one Visiting Day, and it is coming up in two weeks. I am going – but I do not want to see Johnny's father there. I do not think it would be good for Johnny.

A: I notice that the word 'I' comes up very often in your question. Are you interested in what *you want*, or what *Johnny needs*? Have you asked him? Both you and his father do not have to visit at the same time, if you cannot tolerate your ex-husband's presence. Are you certain that only one Visiting Day is allowed? Does the camp present any alternatives for divorced couples? Finally, if nothing else, can you agree with your ex- to divide up the day?

Q: Next week is Parent–Teacher Evening at my son's school. He is eleven years old, and is doing quite well academically. His mother has informed me about this Parent–Teacher Evening. My son has also asked me to come. My girlfriend does not want me to go, however, claiming that this is my ex-'s way of trying to get us back together. What should I do?

A: Your son has indicated to you that he wants you to attend. He is doing well at school, and likely it is important to him that you hear this from his teachers. His mother seems to be helping, in letting you know when this event is taking place – a good step in co-operation, and good for your son too. Your son's teachers should also know that you are interested. It therefore sounds quite important that you attend. You could explain all this to your new girlfriend, and assure her that you will not be 'getting together' again with your ex- as a result of this school meeting. You also have to explore with her why she feels that there is a strong possibility of your getting back together with your ex-. Are there other things in your relationship that make her so insecure in her situation with you? This could be just the tip of the iceberg, the beginning of many resentments your girlfriend may develop toward your son and your ex-spouse.

Q: I recently divorced my husband, who sees our three children (aged seven, nine and eleven) every second Wednesday and every second weekend. He is buying them expensive gifts, and takes them to the cinema, plays and restaurants – which I cannot afford to do. I feel angry and resentful. Should I stop the visits?

A: No, the visits should not stop. You can (a) inform your ex-spouse of the difficulties his actions are causing you and your children, and see if the two of you can come up with other solutions. Tell him you do not wish to get involved in a 'popularity contest' for the children's approval; and (b) examine your own activities with the children. I would hope that you do not complain to them about your inability to provide them with similar luxuries. Instead, point out that there is a difference in lifestyle between the two households, and ask them what you can all do *together* in *your* home to make things as pleasant as possible, while recognising with them that homework still needs to be done, and chores still need to be carried out.

Do not tell them that if they like it better at Dad's place, they can pack their bags. Children can enjoy a walk in the park, a game of Monopoly, a family picnic, etc., as much as a play or a film. It is also a well-known fact that they enjoy the occasional trip to a fast-food restaurant as much as they do a trip to a more exclusive eatery. So relax . . . there is lots you *can* do for them, and with them.

Q: My wife and I separated about a year ago. We have a nine-year-old daughter whom I get to see two evenings per week, and one day at the weekend. My life is such that I have plenty of free time, but my wife is quite busy. When she goes out she hires a sitter, or has a friend to stay with my daughter. Recently when my daughter had to go to the paediatrician, my wife called my father-in-law to take her. I feel that I should be called on such occasions, as I am the father. My wife thinks that I already see enough of our daughter. It is not that my wife and I are fighting, really, but we do not know what is 'best' for our daughter. My daughter and I get along quite well.

A: The added exposure to you would not, from what I have heard, harm your daughter. As a matter of fact, trips to doctors, dentists, etc., are best taken with one of the parents. Assure your ex-wife that you are not trying to take your daughter away from her, that you are not using your daughter to try to be reconciled with her. But also examine why you are not building more of a life for yourself. Do not make the mistake of encouraging your daughter to feel she is the only important person to you, and that she has to fill the voids in your life.

Q: My ex-wife is Catholic and I am Anglican. Since our divorce, she has begun to take the children to her church each Sunday and every holiday. When we were married, we never went to church but did observe festive occasions at home. Now I am beginning to feel I should take the children to my church too, but I wonder if this would confuse them.

A: It seems to me that your religion did not play an important role in your involvement with your children *until* your ex-wife made it an important issue in her own involvement with them. I would think that your children would be best served if you left the issue of religion to your ex-wife, and did not cause this to become an area of further turmoil in your children's lives. If you are really suddenly interested in their religious training, discuss this new area of concern with your ex-wife. You could discuss it with the children as one of the activities that they have while away from you as well; activities in which you are, of course, very interested.

Q: My ex- and I are both Jewish. My parents invite me, along with the children, to celebrate the Holy Days with them. But so do the parents of my ex-. What is the best way of dividing the time? Or should we have two of our four children go with one, and two with the other, and then swap Holy Days each year?

A: I would definitely not split up the children on these occasions. The observance of these festive days are, from the sound of it, family affairs with both your family and your ex-'s family. At a time of family get-togethers, the children tend to be more sensitive to the fact of their parents' divorce; I would not accentuate this by separating the children. Most of the festivals are of more than one day's duration, so if you can, split those days between your family and your ex-'s family. If, however, this involves driving and you do not drive on those holidays, then you may have to alternate the holidays, one being spent with each family in rotation, with a change in arrangements the next year, so that the same festival is spent with the same grandparents every second year.

Q: My ex- and I disagree on who should buy the children's clothes. I feel this is my job as a mother, and the children should know that their mother gets things for them, too. He says that a father can also share in these pleasures. He certainly was not interested in doing that when we were married! Why doesn't he just give me the extra money and let me spend it the way I want to for them?

A: Just because your ex- was mistaken while you were married, and wishes to correct this now, is no reason to deny him the privilege of doing so. This is a time of important interchange with the children and, like most important parts of their lives, should be shared between the two of you. If you are worried about his buying things that the children do not need, or that you have told them they cannot have, you can tell your ex- about this beforehand. This is another area of potential conflict between the two of you, which can be avoided by proper communication.

Q: My seven-year-old son informed me during my last visit that his grandfather told him last week what a terrible person I am, that I have been bad to his Mummy, and that I might be bad to him. He was in tears . . . and I was furious! What should I do? His mother and I have thus far had a good working relationship in dealing with our son.

A: First, I would call your ex- and tell her what you heard from your son, and how upsetting this was to you. If she feels she should handle this with her father, then encourage her to do so. Offer your help, and if it can be arranged that you meet your ex-father-in-law, do not attack him. He is likely to be hurting because you are no longer his daughter's husband, and he is therefore taking up her cause, protecting his daughter. Talk to him about this. Tell him that you understand his feelings, that you as a father would not like to see your child hurt either, and that you therefore would appreciate it if he would offer his criticisms directly to you, not to your son. Do not fight with him, but if his behaviour does not stop, discuss this further with your ex- and check with her whether there is any way she can either curtail your son's visits to his grandfather, or supervise them more directly. If you can do this calmly, you will be helping your son, and will be very deserving of his respect in the future.

Q: I have asked the school principal not to allow my ex-husband to visit our child at school. He refuses to get involved. What should I do?

A: It is unfair to try to make the principal the policeman in this instance. He is right to refuse to be placed in the middle. Your child has a difficult enough task facing your divorce at home and, I am sure, is having enough of a struggle handling school, without the further loss of self-esteem that would result from spreading the fight into the area of his learning, friendships and relationships with teachers.

If your ex- is visiting the school, then he must be feeling left out of this important phase of your child's life. Inform him that these visits, and the conflict surrounding them, are harmful to your child, and that you would like to sit down and discuss your child's schooling, and the role that each of you is to play. Perhaps you could work out an agreement with the principal, so that both of you receive reports and have the chance to visit teachers on a regular basis.

Q: I am planning to be away on vacation for two weeks. This will mean that I miss out on one weekend visit with my children. I have asked my ex- if I could see the children two weekends in a row to make up for the lost time. She has refused. What can I do?

A: If she will not change the schedule, then there really is nothing you *can* do, other than to adjust your vacation time to fit between the two weekends during which you have access. It means shortening your vacation by a few days, but that is the only choice you have.

Remember two things, though. She will eventually have some activity with the children that coincides with one of your access visits. If at that time you can be gracious enough to compromise on her behalf, the chances of her returning the favour in the future will then be increased.

Second, if you decide to forgo your visit to the children this once, remember that you can maintain contact with them while you are away by sending them postcards or letters regularly, thus letting them know where you are and that you are thinking about them. If possible, arrange times that you can call them.

Q: My children keep coming home from weekend visits having forgotten shoes, or other articles of clothing, or books. This aggravates me no end. How can I make my ex- understand how inconvenient this is?

A: First of all, check within yourself your degree of aggravation. Is it only due to the inconvenience of the forgotten articles, or is something going on between you and your ex- which is being played out through the struggle of the forgotten shoes – with your children caught in the middle?

Remember that the children probably have confused feelings about the visits, and this may cause them to be forgetful. Avoid appearing too upset when you discover that articles are missing. Do not harp on the subject. Tell the children that you are concerned about it. Tell your ex- too. See if you can all come up with an idea that would solve the problem. Finally, if this does not work, try setting up a checklist of articles taken, and encourage your ex- and your children to go over this checklist before they return home. Do not be surprised if they lose the checklist! If they do, this may be one of the inconveniences that you have to learn to live with.

Q: When my eight-year-old son comes home from visits to his mother, he has a lot of stories to tell me about what he has done with her and her new boyfriend. I must admit that this makes me jealous, and I do not like to listen to it. Should I tell my son?

A: First, you really have to try to come to terms with these feelings. You are separated, and it sounds to me like your ex- is telling you quite clearly that the two of you are 'through' as husband and wife. By telling you about your ex-'s new boyfriend, your son is also telling you that he is accepting the end of your marriage. You then have to do whatever is necessary – work on it yourself, talk to trusted friends, or try psychotherapy – to set up a new life for yourself. And remember that it is important for your relationship with your son that he be able to share with you as many of his feelings and experiences as possible. This is one of them. He would, I feel, understand if you told him how difficult this is for you, *but* that you are interested in hearing all about it, about *his* feelings about what he does with your ex-wife and her new boyfriend. Do not use him as an informant, though. Let him tell you what he wants to.

Q: Since my separation, I have been going out a lot. Often the girls I am with stay the night. My kids seem to resent having to share their time with my girlfriends. Don't they have to learn the facts of my love life?

A: Yes, your children will have to learn the fact that you have your own life, apart from them, but you have to look at what you are doing to them. If you are seriously dating someone and that new person becomes important in your life – even a possible future wife – then this is something you have to work on with your children. Learn their feelings, introduce them to your new friend, and allow them to establish a relationship. Your partner, I hope, would also be interested in the children, and would have enough time with you to be comfortable about sharing you with the children.

It is an entirely different story if the relationship is a casual one. The girlfriend then would likely want all of your attention during the time she is with you; she would tend to resent the intrusion of your children. Your children would also be put under an extra strain, having to adjust to someone new each time. They might also face the pressure of avoiding talking to each new girlfriend about the other new girlfriend(s). All of this would suggest that you should not introduce them to your 'date' until the relationship is a serious one.

(You should also ask yourself if really you are not feeling some discomfort at being with your children which you might be relieving by adding a third party.)

Q: I have been going out with someone for a long time now. Things are becoming quite serious. How do I introduce him to my children, who are five and seven?

A: Slowly and gradually.

Your children likely know something is going on in your life, having probably sensed your changes in mood as a result of your new relationship. I would begin by telling them that you have been seeing someone, and that you enjoy it. No doubt they will then come up with all kinds of questions about him. Answer those questions as frankly as you can. From this, they will get to 'know' him in a certain way. You can give them a verbal picture of what he is like. (I would also hope that you have done the same with him, telling him about your kids.) Show the children a picture of him.

Next, go for a walk, drive, or have a meal together. Don't rush them, and do not make the meetings too prolonged. You will soon be able to judge how they are getting on, and let nature take its course.

Allow all of them (children and boyfriend) to talk to you about their feelings and reactions towards each other. But do not take it upon yourself to be the only one working towards fostering their relationship. Allow them to do it too.

Q: My boyfriend has met my children. They get along well. He has three children of his own, whom he sees every second weekend, and every Wednesday night. Now we want to introduce the children to each other. How?

A: First, remember that left to their own devices, children usually will get along quite well, unless there are major differences between them.

I would follow the same slow, gradual route outlined in the previous question, recognising that now the situation is slightly more complicated, and you have to deal with that many more permutations and combinations. The children will also be checking closely for possible favouritism, etc. This will require additional time and patience. Listen, be patient, and once again allow nature to take its course. I have seen many situations in which the children take over and develop close and wonderful friendships that actually *help* the 'new stepfamily' to meld.

One more caution. Do not, once they meet, force them to have to meet each and every time. They may want – on both sides – to have 'both of you' or 'one of you' to themselves occasionally.

Q: Today was cold, and my ex- had our daughter for the day. I am sure that he did not make her wear her hat to school, and she will probably catch a cold. When I call him to tell him how to dress her, he resents it. How do I get him to co-operate? My daughter is eleven.

A: You will not get him to co-operate by calling and telling him how to dress your daughter. You will not get your daughter to co-operate by telling her how to dress. Your daughter should have the common sense to look after herself in the cold. She needs to feel that you respect her ability to care for herself. If you have been able to work with her as a young child to the point that she recognises her physical needs, and respects them, then by now you should allow her to take over.

In the same vein, if you make your ex- feel that without your call he would not know how to care for your daughter, he too is likely to react angrily, and resent your calling. You have to work towards allowing yourself to step back a bit and let your daughter grow up. An additional point: remember that if your daughter does not want to wear the hat, she'll take it off as soon as she's out of sight of either you or your ex- anyway!

Two useful guidelines to help you judge when it is appropriate to call and remind your ex- about something like this are (a) how receptive is he? (b) if he were your child's schoolteacher, would you call him with a reminder about this issue?

Q: My ex- and I still cannot tolerate the sight of each other. Each time I come to pick up the children, we get into a horrible fight. Name-calling, slapping around ... the works. The kids are seven, eleven and twelve. I am sure this is going to harm them.

A: Have you tried sitting down with a neutral person such as a conciliator and working on 'growing up' to the point of being able to behave civilly to one another? You state that you know – and I am sure both of you know – that this is harmful to the children, and yet you persist!

Okay, then, if you cannot stop, what you have to do is find a substitute to pick up and deliver your children. In time, maybe things will cool off enough for you to be able to do this for yourself again. Also, if you live close to each other, your twelve-year-old will soon be able to take the responsibility of taking the younger siblings along (unless, of course, by that time, the twelve-year-old is tired of watching this nonsense and does not wish to see either one of you!).

Q: I have heard that my ex- is a homosexual, and I think it is true. I do not mind my daughter visiting him, but I am worried about my son. I do not think his dad should have access to him. What if his influence encourages my son to become homosexual? And what about the possibility that he might molest my son?

A: I will not question your source of information, or its validity. However, even if your husband *is* homosexual, this does *not* mean he is rendered ineffectual as a parent, or that he is incapable of properly parenting your son. Nor does it mean that he will 'teach' your son to be a homosexual, or 'seduce' him.

The fact that one is a homosexual does not make one a child molester. I have found that homosexuals who have married and have had children are usually people who have considerable conflict about their homosexuality, and would like to spare their children similar pain and conflict. The odds are good that your husband will do his utmost to guide your son *away from* this problem.

However, if your husband is *known* to be a child molester, or has previously involved his own children in his homosexual activities, then the picture changes drastically. I have stated often that there are very few reasons for denying a parent access to his children. THIS IS ONE OF THEM! Use every legal means of denying him access – at least until he obtains professional help from a competent person who can then let you know when it is safe to resume visits. If the children benefit – in your opinion and theirs – from seeing their father, then *always make certain* that someone whom you trust completely – the court welfare officer for instance – accompanies the children on all visits, and that that person takes all precautions necessary to ensure their safety.

Q: My ex- and I have discussed splitting the children. We have joint custody of six children, aged four to sixteen, and we can communicate quite well. What we have thought of is almost like musical chairs, but allows the children to be together in various combinations for two weeks at a time, with all the kids being together every second weekend. It involves a lot of shifting, but we have worked on the logistics and it does seem feasible. Would it do them any emotional harm?

A: Wow! You certainly have worked on this 'project'. A lot of thought and planning has evidently gone into it – it begins to make me wonder what caused you to split up. Anyway, confusing though your scheme may sound, I would predict that it would not do any emotional harm to the children.

Although one would have to worry about the lack of stability of relationships in such an arrangement, that would be dismissed due to the stability of all the 'planned and organised' changes. In other words, there exists a consistent pattern to all this change. Further, such a situation – indeed, almost any situation – is tolerable as long as there is consistent, on-going interest and emotional support on the part of each parent. This factor certainly appears to be there in your case. The children can get to know each other better in the smaller groups, too, than in the confusion of six at a time.

I do not view this as 'splitting the children', I feel that any family of six should arrange for regular times when you have groups of two or three children alone for a day or two, as far as that may be feasible. Good luck with your arrangement!

Q: My six-year-old daughter is having her birthday this Sunday. This is one of her father's weekends for access. I think it is highly unfair that she should spend that day with him, that he give her a party, and that I – who cares for her most of the time – cannot celebrate her birthday with her.

A: At this age, we rarely see the birthday party held on the actual date of the birthday. In my experience, most six-year-olds are used to a small party or gift-receiving on the actual date, with a bigger party held on the nearest weekend. So how about allowing your six-year-old to enjoy her birthday without the guilt feeling that this enjoyment is interfering with *your* sense of fair play, by (a) having a little party for her and her friends the week before or after, and (b) letting her tell you how much she enjoyed her special day, even if it was with her Daddy. Do not make big problems out of little ones!

Q: My wife and I have been divorced for four years. We have a sixteen-year-old son and a twelve-year-old daughter. I have very liberal access; my children and I see each other at least twice a week, and we get along quite well. My ex- and I have learned to co-operate in parenting. Now I have had an excellent offer to advance myself in my career. The only problem is that it involves a transfer to a town a thousand miles away from here. What should I do?

A: You claim that you have a good relationship with your children, and with your ex-. You must, therefore, be putting a great deal of time and effort into this relationship with them. This is something you will obviously be unable to do from a distance of a thousand miles.

I am sure it would be impossible to talk your ex- into moving to this remote town too. Let's assume that it is. So you have to sit down and measure the pros and cons of the issue. How damaging to your career would it be to postpone the move for four or five years, or to refuse the transfer completely? How much will you resent your children for 'holding you back' if you do not make the move? Or can you arrange it financially so that they can visit you every second weekend, or once a month, and you do the same? How well can you communicate with each other on the phone (though it is never as satisfying)?

Sit down with your children, and with your ex-, and talk over the various possibilites. The final decision is still yours. Remember that your children need your guidance at this stage, but they need sensible guidance. Should you pass up the transfer, only to resent the children and become depressed, then you will not have been nearly as good a father to them as you could be a thousand miles away, contented in your career, happy with yourself, and still trying to be with your children as much as possible.

You also have to be aware of the fact that in a few years they will be much more independent, and you want to make sure that you will not be throwing your decision back at them and trying to hold them more closely to you than you should.

It is a tough decision, and I have tried to set out some of the factors that you should take into account, but in the end . . . the decision is yours.

10 Questions Children Often Ask Me

Q: Mum and Dad are getting a divorce, and they are asking me what I *really* want; which one do I want to stay with? I do not know how to answer them. What should I do?

A: All children feel guilty about making a choice between mother and father . . . between two parents you love. This is why such a question is unreasonable and should not have been asked of you. However, if you have been asked this question you will have to try to recognise that *you* did not bring about this situation – your parents did. You are not taking something away from them; they took something from you by getting divorced. Of course one of them will feel sad if you tell them you want to live with the other parent. But that is *their* problem, not yours. They will have to work out their feelings and come to terms with their sadness. Do not answer that question. Instead, point out, if possible, how difficult they make it for you by making you choose. Remind them that you need shelter, a stable environment, a place where you can do things you have been doing up until now (school, sports, etc.), a home in which there will be love, yes, but also security, attention to your needs . . . and even discipline.

Remember, too, that even if you are not living with one of your parents, you will still be able to see that parent and do things with that parent. And this is something you should talk about with *both* parents. If you enjoy going to a movie with your mother, but prefer going to a football game with your father, tell them this – this can still happen, no matter which parent you are actually living with.

Above all, do not blame yourself for this situation. It is not your fault. If you blame yourself, you are only being unfair – to yourself.

Q: Mummy told Daddy to leave because they were fighting so much. I am not getting along so well with Mummy now either. I am worried she may ask me to leave too.

A: Most children whose parents have separated have exactly the same feelings you do. I can understand why you feel that way. You saw your Daddy and Mummy fighting, and then your Daddy left. Now you and your Mummy are sometimes fighting – and you wonder if this means you will have to leave, just like your Daddy did.

You should understand that there are big differences between how two adults feel about each other, and how parents feel about children. It seems that the feelings of adults towards each other can change quite a lot over the years – that is why there are so many divorces. But between parents and children, the feelings of love do not change that much. When the children are young, the need of the children for the parents and the parents for the children are strong enough to keep them together, even if they do fight once in a while. When you do leave the home, it will be because you are old enough and mature enough to be out on your own.

By the way, most children like you, whose parents are getting a divorce, find themselves either fighting with the parent who has remained in the home, or being too frightened to fight at all. They are afraid – just as you are – that they are going to be left by their parents. The best thing you can do is to discuss with your mother what you are really afraid of. Maybe then the two of you will be able to understand each other better, and be more comfortable with one another.

Q: My Mum tells us children that Daddy left the house because we were always fighting. Can that be true?

A: No, most likely it is not true. Parents do not leave each other because the children are fighting or misbehaving. They leave each other because they no longer love each other and cannot get along well enough to continue living together.

Maybe your Mother is telling you this because she is trying to get you to stop fighting. I know it is normal for children to fight sometimes. Maybe you are fighting a lot, though, and if you are, it is probably because there is a lot of tension in your house. Could it be that you have picked up some of the tension that existed between your parents? It sounds to me like all of you should get together with your mother – and, if possible, your father too – and talk over the real reasons for your parents' separation, and for the fighting that is going on between you children.

Q: I used to invite my friends over to my house to stay the night. Now my parents have separated and I am ashamed to have my friends over. So now I am feeling really lonely, and am scared that I am going to lose my friends.

A: Your parents' separation is no cause for shame. Their separation has nothing to do with you, or anything you have done wrong. These feelings of shame you have are feelings that should be talked over with your parents. I hope they will help you understand that you are not to blame for what has happened.

Another thing to remember is that your friends, if they are really worthwhile friends, should not condemn you for the misfortune of your parents' splitting up. They would probably like to talk to you about it, though, but they don't know if you are ready or willing to do so. The best way to deal with this is to tell them what has happened, and talk to them about it. Then go right ahead and invite your friends for an overnight stay.

Q: Whenever I visit my mother, she seems to have a different 'friend' over at her apartment. This bothers me a lot, and stops me sleeping. I do not want to tell my father about it, but I think I have decided not to visit her any more.

A: You are not being fair to yourself, or to your mother, if you stop visiting her without telling her why. Just tell her that her 'friend's' being at the apartment bothers you, and that you would like to spend more time with her alone. If she refuses to co-operate, then you can tell her you would like to stop the visits unless she changes.

Q: I am eleven. I have a four-year-old brother. I see my Dad every second weekend, but my brother always comes along. We end up spending most of the time looking after my brother. I would like to do other things with my Dad instead.

A: Why don't you tell your parents this? Maybe they could change some of the visits so that you could be alone with your

Dad – say every second visit or so. Then your brother could be alone with him on the other visits. This would give you a chance to spend time alone with both your parents.

Q: I am a six-year-old boy. My Mummy and Daddy separated a little while ago. Since then, I have been wetting my bed at night. This really bothers me. I don't know what to do.

A: Quite often, young boys and girls whose Mummy or Daddy leave home start to do things that they used to do when they were younger. This only lasts for a little while, and usually goes away. You say this bothers you, and I can understand why. But I am sure you are even more bothered by the fact that your *Daddy* has left the house, and you cannot do anything about it. Can you talk to your Mummy and Daddy, and tell them how mad and sad you are about what has happened? You probably will not be able to get your Mummy and Daddy back together, but sometimes just telling them how you feel will make you feel much better – and perhaps stop you from wetting your bed.

Q: Every time Dad calls and makes plans to visit us, he doesn't show up. I am beginning to think he does not love my sister and me the same as he does not love our Mum. Do you think I am right?

A: Most of the time when parents split up, it is because they have somehow stopped loving each other. But it is very, very unusual for a parent to stop loving his children!

Quite often, parents who leave the home end up feeling quite ashamed, and guilty for the hurt this causes to their children. Most of them try to make up to their children for this by being an even better parent than before.

But sometimes, a parent feels so bad that he just does not think he can even *face* his children any more. Parents like this are worried that their children will condemn them. What they really want most is for their children to forgive them – but they do not know how to ask.

Parents like this also worry that they have to be such 'super parents', that a plain old regular visit – to the park, to the zoo, or just having a snack and talking – is not good enough. They feel that maybe they have to do things that they really cannot afford.

Why not call your Dad on the phone and tell him you are not looking for 'super' visits – it is *him* that you love, and *him* you want to see. If he still does not come around, then it means he is having a difficult time dealing with himself, and finding it impossible to see you at this time. This is going to be hard for you to deal with, and the only thing I can suggest is to call him or write to him and tell him that if and when he is ready to visit you, you will be happy to see him.

Maybe he will eventually come around. But just remember that his staying away is not *your* fault. If you find that you keep thinking it is your fault, and you start getting down on yourself, talk to your mother about seeing someone who can talk to you about these feelings.

Q: We used to spend a lot of time with Mum's parents. They were our favourite grandparents until Mum 'took off'. Now I do not feel like spending any time with them. Dad does, and so does my brother. Why should I?

A: You said it yourself: they were your favourite grandparents. They must have deserved that title! Now your mother has left, though, and you no longer want to spend time with them. Are you angry with them because your mother left? What did they have to do with it? Or more likely, are you angry with your mother and, not being able to tell her so, you take it out on them? That could be the reason.

Another reason could be that whenever you are with your grandparents, it makes you remember your mother. This makes you sad, so you have decided not to visit your grandparents. Still another reason: maybe you are feeling sad and hurt by your mother's leaving, and you can't stand being with someone who might change this mood.

There can be many reasons why you no longer wish to visit these grandparents, but it sounds like they have not changed their attitude towards *you*. I would suggest two things:

(a) Talk to your father and brother – and maybe even your grandparents – about your hurt, sad, angry feelings. Maybe they can help you understand these feelings.

(b) Take a sheet of plain white paper. Put a line down the middle. On one side, put the reasons why you do not want to visit your grandparents, and what you do not like about them.

On the other side, write down why you would want to visit them, and what you do like about them. By the time you get into this second list, you will probably find that you are once again feeling a lot like visiting them! Give them the chance to continue to be good grandparents to you, even though your mother has, for reasons of her own, chosen to 'take off'.

Q: Whenever I play cricket, or am in the school play or something special like that, my parents fight about who can come and watch. I would really like them both to come, even if they bring their 'new friends'. How can I get this across to them?

A: First, you have to sit down with each one of them separately – or if you can, better still, get them together. Tell them exactly how you feel. It sounds to me as if you would rather they both showed up and watched you, than continue to fight about which one should come. Tell them that, clearly and forcefully. Ask them who decided that they could not all show up together, and who is supposed to benefit by it? Suggest to them that they can sit in different sections of the arena or auditorium.

It seems that you are having to settle some of these arguments between them. You may feel that this is unfair on you – and it is. On the other hand, it may help you do a better job of dealing with people in the future!

One more thing. They are bound to argue about who takes you there and brings you home. You could suggest coming with one, and leaving with the other, or taking turns on alternate occasions. And if they absolutely *cannot* be together in the same place on the same evening, they will just have to go back to attending on alternate occasions. Do your best.

Helpful Addresses to Contact

1. Family Institute
   105, Cathedral Road, Cardiff, S. Wales
   Tel 0222/26532
2. Institute of Family Therapy (London)
   43, New Cavendish Street, London W.1
   Tel. 01/935/1651
3. National Family Conciliation Council
   34, Milton Road, Swindon. Wilts SN1 5JA
   (for address of local Conciliation Service)
   Tel 0793/618486
4. National Marriage Guidance Council
   Herbert Grey College
   Little Church Street, Rugby CV21 3AP
   (for address of local Marriage Guidance Service)
5. Scottish Conciliation Service
   127 Rose Street, South Lane, Edinburgh
   (for address of local Conciliation Service)
   Tel 031/226/4507
6. Stepfamily
   162 Tenison Road, Cambridge
   (for general information and address of local self help
   group)
   Counselling Service Tel. 0223/460313
   (7 a.m. to 10 p.m., except Saturdays)

Index

children – *cont.*
  in non-peaceful separation,
    34–38
  normal developmental problems
    of, 8–9, 29, 55–57, 75–76,
    102–103
  parental role assumed by, 29,
    32–33, 34, 99–102, 132–34
  in peaceful separation, 25–34
  secrecy requested by, 82–84,
    108–109, 143–46
  visits feared by, 74–76
  young, 8–9, 10, 54–55, 137–38
continuity of parenthood:
  breaking the news and, 7–8,
    13–14, 16–17;
  in custodial arrangements, 49,
    55–56
  misbehaviour and, 108–110
  new relationships and, 113–15,
    116–17
  parent–child fighting and,
    178–80
  in separation period, 25–26
  visits and, 56–57, 62–63, 77–78,
    79–80
control, children's need for,
    103–104
control, parent's, over influences
    on children, 81, 129–31,
    173–74
co-operation between parents:
  campers' Visitors Day and,
    93–95, 165–66
  children's feelings about dating
    and, 118–19
  children's illnesses and, 95–96
  children's manipulative
    behaviour and, 31, 140–41
  children's misbehaviour and,
    33, 87, 88–90, 109–110,
    143–44, 149–50
  children's regular routine and,
    84–85
  children's sharing with both
    parents and, 56–58, 108–109
  in custodial arrangements,
    53–54

ex-spouse's refusal of. *See* unco-
    operative behaviour, ex-
    spouse's
  girlfriend's/boyfriend's
    opposition to, 165–67
  in peaceful separation, 19–20,
    21–22
  rights respected in, 20–22, 29
  sexual attraction during, 120–21
    co-parenting, 51–54, 175–76;
    negative side of, 52–53
    success rate of, 53
custodial arrangements, 50–61,
    165–66;
  changing, 125–26
  extra visits in, 167–68
  job transfers and, 176–77
  'middle man' as option in, 52,
    173–75
  parenting improved in, 53–54,
    123–25, 168–69
  splitting up children in, 175–76
  types of, 50–53
  varying alliances in, 55–57
  See also visits
Custody suits, 10–11, 41–49;
  appropriate circumstances for,
    45–47
  children excluded from, 44–46
  children harmed by, 36–37,
    38–39, 41–46, 48–49
  children protected by, 36–37,
    45–49
  children's preferences in, 30,
    42–44, 47–48, 178–79
  children's reality distorted by,
    43–45
  children's vs. adults' welfare in,
    43–45
  'friendly chat' in judge's
    chambers during, 42
  lawyers' effect on, 38–40
  mediation in, 41–42, 49
  motives in, 38–39, 45–47
  parenting ability eroded by,
    43–45
  rational control lost in, 44
cynicism, 159–60

refusals to rearrange visits and,
169–71

illnesses, children's, 89–91, 95–96
infants, 8–9, 164
infidelity, 10–11, 46–47
'information overload,' 54

joint custody, 51–52

'Kramer versus Kramer', 44–45

lawyers, attitudes and goals of,
39–40, 128–29
Leroy family, 131–34
loneliness, ex-spouse's, 111–12
loss, ex-spouse's feelings of, 23–25,
111–12

McDonald family, 124–25
McNaughton family, 10
marriage:
divorce as breakdown in
parenting vs., 17, 27–28
euphoria associated with, 112
Mason family, 10
maturity, pseudo-, in children,
32–33, 99–102
Menninger, Karl, 160
mental health, expressing
emotions and, 8–9
Mike, 97, 98–99, 101–103
moving, 57–61;
coping technique for, 59–61
after re-marriage, 156–59

needs, children's:
for control, 103–104
in visits, 85–86, 180–81
needs, parent's:
in breaking the news to
children, 7

children's needs vs., 7–8
to explain decision to divorce,
3–4

overachieving behaviour,
children's, 98–111

parent, custodial (at home):
with apathetic ex-spouse,
134–35, 180–81
children's fighting with, 177–80
children's misbehaviour and,
103–109, 110
children's relationship with
outside parent accepted by,
63–64, 80–81, 104–105,
124–25, 164–65
day-to-day responsibilities of,
25–26, 27–28
initial issues for, 23–34
intervention of, in visits, 81–84
new relationship of, 113–16,
118–20
outside parent as threat to,
64–67, 123–25
outside parent's needs respected
by, 20–22, 29
refusal of, to rearrange visits,
169–71
in separation period, 23–34
visiting arrangements and tips
for, 79–84, 86–90, 173–74
parent, non-custodial (outside):
children encouraged to share
with, 56–58, 108–109
children's individual needs and,
84–86, 180–81
custodial parent undermined
by, 63–64, 64–67, 80–81,
87–88
ex-spouse's re-marriage as
threat to, 149–51, 154–56
increased interest of, in
parenting, 123–25, 168–69
initial issues for, 19–23
job transfers and, 176–77

non-custodial parent's access
  denied after, 164–65
sex life in, 152–53
surname change in, 152–53
time span between divorce and,
  147–48
wedding ceremony for, 154
Rosenberg family, 126–28

Sarah, 97, 100–102
school, 97–110;
  being considered different in,
    98–100, 103, 107–108,
    143–46
  boarding school, 105–106
  children's need for control in,
    103
  children's relationship with
    adults in, 97–98
  'early warning system' for
    problems in, 105
  extra-curricular activities in, 96,
    182–83
  friends alienated in, 98,
    99–102
  grades in, 108–109
  overachievement in, 98, 99–102
  parent–teacher consultations in,
    105
  re-marriage and, 154–56
  visiting arrangements and,
    107–108, 170, 182–83
secrecy, children's requests for,
  82–84, 108–109, 143–46
security: children's need for, 7, 13,
  16–17, 25, 49, 55–57, 77–78,
  78–79, 108–110, 113–15,
  116–17, 178–80;
  parents' childhood memories
    and, 59–60
  'tough guy' image in, 101–103
self-doubt, ex-spouse's surrender
  to, 159–60
self-esteem: children's loss of,
  42–43, 113–14;
  exhaustion and, 103–105
  parents' encouragement and,
    107–109

self-esteem, parent's loss of,
  23–24, 112–13
self-examination, self-
  condemnation vs., 161–62
separation: non-peaceful, 34–40;
  children's mixed feelings in,
    34–36
  court compromises in, 39–40
  marital relationship prolonged
    in, 38
  parent's feelings in, 35–38
  positive side of, 34–35
  reconciliation feared in, 39–40
  visitation in, 35–38
separation: separation period,
  19–40;
  children's adjustment time in,
    34
  children's regressive behaviour
    in, 31–34
  for outside parent, 19–23
  patience needed in, 27–29,
    30–31, 33, 37
  peaceful, 19–34
  for remaining parent, 23–34
sexual relations, 101–103;
  with ex-spouse, 120–21
  flaunting, 112–13, 119–21
  homosexual, 131–32, 174–76
  promiscuous, 131–32
  after re-marriage, 151–53
solicitors, 38–40, 128
Stone family, 10

teenagers. *See* adolescents
Thompson, Chris, 1–4
Tina, 2–5
Tommy, 75

unco-operative behaviour, ex-
  spouse's, 122–36;
  as extremely harmful, 130–32
  calm approach to, 125–26
  categories of, 123–24
  custodial arrangements changed
    due to, 125–30

unco-operative behaviour – *cont.*
  increased interest in parenting
    as, 123–25, 168–69
  lack of punctuality in visiting as,
    124–26
  refusals to rearrange visits as,
    169–71

vacations, 89–91, 92–94
  children's preferences in, 93–94
  visits rearranged for, 169–71
values: parents' disagreement on,
    46–47;
  in discipline techniques, 88–91
  fitness as parents and, 46–47
    131–32, 174–76
  integrity vs. hypocrisy in,
    129–30
  religious, 92–93, 167–68
vengeance:
  lawyer hired for, 38–39
  outside parent's fear of, 20–22,
    29–30
  visitation used in, 36–38
visits, 62–96;
  apathetic outside parent in,
    134–36, 180–82
  arguments over, 70–75
  attention paid to children
    during, 86–87
  for birthday parties, 89–91,
    93–95, 175–77
  children's excitement before,
    77–78
  children's experiences
    emphasised after, 80–81
  children's fear of, 74–76,
    144–45
  children's friends allowed on, 55
  children's illnesses and, 95–96
  children's individual needs in,
    84–86, 180–81
  children's regular routine and,
    84–85, 107–108
  complex potentials of, 62–63,
    78–79

continuity of parenthood
    established in, 63, 77
  custodial parent's intervention
    in, 81–84
  custodial parent's view of,
    64–67
  dates made for, 54–56, 86–88
  dating while, 116–17
  discipline problems due to,
    76–79
  divorce anxieties involved in,
    63–64, 78–79, 123
  divorce case discussed in, 87–89
  exaggeration of aspects in,
    67–71
  extra, 166–68
  harmful events in, 37, 81–84,
    130–32
  job transfers and, 176–77
  marital tension relieved in,
    66–67, 68–70, 122–23,
    170–71, 173–75
  'middle man' used in, 52–53,
    173–75
  outside parent seen as threat in,
    64–67
  to outside parent's home, 85–87
  outside parent's view of, 67–71
  parenting as emphasis of, 78–80
  parents' communication in,
    73–74, 79–81, 82, 86–91
  planning for, 83–84, 86–88,
    107–108
  punctuality in, 124–26
  religious holidays and, 89–93,
    167–69
  school routine and, 96, 107–108,
    169–70, 182–83
  on special occasions, 89–96,
    167–69, 175–77
  to summer camp, 93–95,
    165–66
  transition phase in, 79–80

Wilson family, 123–24